Whatever
Happened
to
TRUTH

by

ANTHONY M. CONIARIS

Light & Life Publishing Company
Minneapolis, Minnesota
www.light-n-life.com

Light & Life Publishing Company
Minneapolis, MN
www.light-n-life.com

Copyright © 2001
Second Printing Copyright © 2023
Anthony M. Coniaris

Library of Congress Control Number: 2001133104

All rights reserved. No part of this book may be repro-
duced, stored in a retrieval system, or transmitted in any
form or by any means, electronic, mechanical, photo-
copying, recording, or otherwise without the written
permission of Light & Life Publishing Company.

ISBN No. 978-1-880971-68-0

Table of Contents

Dedicated to the parishioners of St. Mary's Greek Orthodox Church in Minneapolis, Minnesota, whom I served as a presbyter for forty-four years.

Whatever Happened to Truth?

Following are some facts about what has happened to truth.

Fact Number One:

In 1935, psychologists from thirty nations met in Germany to conclude that war was normal and good because of Darwin's philosophy of the survival of the fittest!

Fact Number Two:

In 1975, the American Psychological Association met to pronounce that homosexuality was no longer deviant but acceptable behavior.

Fact Number Three:

In 1998, a number of psychologists appeared on a national TV show to declare that adulterous affairs between married persons were not harmful but even useful.

Fact Number Four:

In 1998, the Journal of the American Psychological Association published the results of a study that argued that sex between adults and children (pedophilia) is not always harmful and that so-called "willing encounters" should be relabeled as "adult-child sex."

Fact Number Five:

In his book Dancing Alone, Frank Schaeffer describes what has happened to truth in America:

The communists showed the Orthodox Church the respect of putting some of its faithful adherents against a wall and shooting them. However backhanded that "compliment," at least it implied that religious faith mattered enough to kill, or imprison people for. In America, in our pluralistic culture through which all religion has been diminished to mere interdenominational squabbling or "personalized" religiosity, there is a more deadly and insidious form of execution being performed daily against the Orthodox faithful; religion has been relegated to a nether world of irrelevance! The message of the American knowledge class is not, "we will shoot you for your faith," but rather "your faith does not matter. There is no such thing as truth. It's all just a matter of personal opinion." *

---

* *Dancing Alone.* Frank Schaeffer. HCO Press. Brookline, MA 1994

Charles Colson at Yale

Fact Number Six:

Charles Colson tells of being invited to speak at Yale Law School in 1996 where a group of fearless Christian students had organized a forum to address the provocative question of how Yale had contributed to undermining the rule of law. For, it was at Yale that Critical Legal Studies was born, a deconstructionist movement to strip the law of any objective meaning.

Colson planned to address that issue from a Christian point of view and he wondered if the meeting might erupt into a riot.

A sympathetic Yale professor told him not to worry. "When these kids come to Yale," he said, "they are taught that the law has nothing to do with morality And they accept that. So you can have your opinions, and they'll find those interesting, but they won't even bother to argue."

And that is exactly what happened. They listened politely, took a few notes, then packed up their papers and quietly slipped out of the auditorium.

Looking back at the experience, Colson said, "Debate can be unpleasant at times, but at least it presupposes that there are truths worth defending. In our postmodernist world, however, your truths are yours, my truths are mine, and none are significant enough to get passionate about. And if there is no truth, then we cannot persuade one another by rational arguments. All that's left is sheer power—which opens the door to a new form of fascism."

More on What is Happening to Truth Today

F ollowing is more about what is happening to truth today.

Fact Number Seven:

If, for example, you oppose the killing of innocent, helpless unborn babies today, you are labeled as a cruel, unthinking extremist. However, if you support the murders of these babies through abortion, the world will call you enlightened, caring and "pro-choice." Advocates of abortion cannot bring themselves to say "choose abortion" or even "choose to terminate a pregnancy" so they say simply, "choose."

Fact Number Eight:

If you say that Jesus is "the Way, the Truth, and the Life," that is, that He is the only way to God, because He is Himself the One true God, the world will not hesitate to call you unenlightened, intolerant, and a fanatic. If, on the other hand, you say that there are many ways to God (and thus call Jesus a liar), you are called broad-minded and tolerant.

Fact Number Nine:

If you challenge dishonest practices in the workplace, they will call you a whistleblower and a trouble-maker. But if you go along with the dishonesty and help cover it up, they will bless you and call you "one of the boys" and "a good team player."

What does Jesus say to this? When you are persecuted because of righteousness, He says, you are blessed because it is proof that you are in God's kingdom; it is proof that you are His disciples; it is proof that you are in the company of the prophets, apostles and martyrs.

Why do I mention all these facts? Because they all make me wonder, "Whatever happened to truth?"

So, let us discuss truth—the truth that is the same yesterday, today, and forever; the truth that saves; the truth that sets us free; the truth that is being denied and distorted today perhaps as never before. Specifically our subject is, "Whatever happened to truth?"

The Prophet Isaiah foretold what would happen to truth when he wrote centuries ago, "Woe to them that call evil good and good evil; that put darkness for light, and light for darkness; that put bitter for sweet, and sweet for bitter" (Isaiah 5:20).

Distorting Truth

What is behind the distortion of truth today? One factor is the distortion that has occurred in the meaning of words. Communication in our generation is characterized by bizarre distortions in the meaning of words. Beneath such word distortions lies a more serious moral problem, an inability to make distinctions between good and evil, right and wrong, light and darkness. Or, as in the case of the politically correct movement today, it is a deliberate attempt to deny the existence of objective truth.

The reason for the moral insanity in Isaiah's day was that the people had turned their backs on God and despised His word.

Is not the same happening today?

We Christians need to recapture the language of our faith in order to rescue words from what C.S. Lewis once called "verbicide"—the murder of words and their meaning and thus, ultimately, the destruction of the truth behind these words.

One clergyman, the Rev. Joe Wright, described what has happened to truth in a prayer he offered to open the new session of the Kansas Senate. He prayed:

> *Heavenly Father, we come before you today to ask Your forgiveness and to seek Your direction and guidance. We know Your Word says, 'Woe to those who call evil good,' but that is exactly what we have done. We have lost our spiritual equilibrium and*

reversed our values. We confess that we have ridiculed the absolute truth of Your Word and called it pluralism. We have worshiped other gods and called it multiculturalism. We have endorsed perversion and called it alternative lifestyle...We have polluted the air with profanity and pornography and called it freedom of expression.

By murdering the meaning of words, we murder truth. Couples, for example, used to "shack up," now they "cohabit."

Daniel Patrick Moynihan has given us the phrase "defining deviancy down" to describe a process by which we change the meaning of morality to fit what we are doing.

Facing the Truth

One day a committee called on President Lincoln to discuss a national problem. Their case was built mostly on "supposings," suppose this… suppose that. After listening for a while Lincoln said, "How many legs would a sheep have if you called its tail a leg?" "Five," they said. "No, it would only have four," Lincoln said. "Calling a tail a leg doesn't make it one." Giving something a new name does not change it. Calling falsehood a "white lie" doesn't make it less a lie.

The first step in solving a problem is to admit that one has a problem, that is, to admit the truth. Then it means calling it by its proper name. It means saying, "I made a mistake… I didn't tell the truth… I cheated. I lied…"

That is what David—a man after God's own heart— did. He told the Lord, "I finally admitted all my sins to You and stopped trying to hide them… And You forgave me" (Psalm 32:5).

St. Paul admitted the truth when he called himself "the foremost of sinners."

"Humankind cannot bear very much reality," said the poet T.S. Eliot.

We need not look far for proof of this statement. People flee from reality, from truth, using escape routes that range from drugs and alcohol to political correctness, from denial and rationalization to blaming each other for their faults. Healing for the alcoholic begins with the admission of the truth: "I am an alcoholic."

"You shall know the truth, and the truth shall make you free," said Jesus. But you must do more than know the truth; you must admit it; you must confess it; you must assume responsibility for it. Facing the truth is essential to repentance and recovery.

Christ is the truth that sets us free—free from delusions, free from the many false ideas and images about ourselves and others.

Indeed, Christ is the Truth Who liberates.

St. Ambrose identified truth with Christ when he wrote,

When we speak about wisdom, we are speaking of Christ.

When we speak about virtue, we are speaking of Christ.

When we speak about justice, we are speaking of Christ.

When we speak about peace, we are speaking of Christ.

When we speak about truth and life and redemption, we are speaking of Christ.

Define Your Terms

O ne of the first principles of logic is that we must begin by defining our terms. Exactly what do the words we use mean? Do they mean one thing to us and something else to the one with whom we're conversing?

For, you see, we can so easily distort the meaning of words. We can make them mean whatever we want them to mean. We can make up our own definitions to suit ourselves.

Lewis Carroll described this phenomenon a long time ago when he put these words in the mouth of Humpty Dumpty: "When I use a word, it means just what I choose it to mean—neither more nor less."

Malcolm Muggeridge wrote:

> One of the things that appalls me and saddens me about the world today is the condition of words. Words can be polluted even more dramatically and drastically than rivers and land and sea. There has been a terrible destruction of words in our time... Without words we are hopeless and defenseless; their misuse is our undoing.

When words lose their objective meaning, then all values, including truth itself, can be toppled. This has now happened.

No God - No Truth

Dostoevsky said once, "If there is no God, everything is permissible."

The premise of our secular world is that there is no God.

One important reason for believing in God, by the way, is that you are acknowledging that you are not God.

If there is no God, then there is no absolute truth. If there is no God, then there is only the individual. And each individual defines his own words and makes up his own truth. Each individual becomes pope and king. Each individual becomes the supreme court. Truth is what each individual says it is, and any attempt to suggest otherwise is a violation of individual freedom.

Thus, John Locke's Enlightenment theory of "the right of private judgment" has become the essence of "true religion."

And we now have, as a result, thousands of Christian "denominations," each based on private judgment, private interpretation of the Bible. Some Protestant denominations, for example, teach predestination, i.e., God arbitrarily decides who is to be saved and damned regardless of what a person does. Other denominations teach that God respects the free will He gave us and allows us to choose freely the gift of salvation. He wants all to be saved. It is obvious that these denominations do not believe in the same God.

Yet because each belief is the product of "the right of private judgment" each is considered "true religion."

Such private interpretation renders truth relative. It is as if God alters His truth to accommodate the subjective beliefs of each individual. Thus, we have "Christian" denominations denying the reality of absolute truth about God.

It is as the Prophet Isaiah described when he said, "All we like sheep have gone astray; we have turned every one to his own way" (Is. 53:6).

Nihilism

The denial of absolute truth leads to nihilism. Nihilism is the belief that there is no absolute truth, that all truth is relative.

The heart of this philosophy was expressed most clearly by Nietzsche and by a character of Dostoevsky in the phrase: "God is dead, therefore man becomes God and everything is permissible."

"Everything permissible" includes lying, cheating, rape, murder and every other rapacious behavior imaginable It includes the holocausts of the twentieth century. The Armenian holocaust. The Nazi holocaust of six million Jews, Gypsies and others. The Soviet holocaust of 60 million murdered by the Communists, mostly for their Christian faith.

If God is dead, and man becomes god, all these tragedies are permissible. They have happened and can happen again.

The Truth and Freud

An example of such a nihilist was Sigmund Freud, who wrote *The Future of an Illusion* in 1927. Freud held that religion was a psychological crutch that held together weak individuals who could not face reality or truth.

He argued that God was but an illusion created by infantile adults who refused to "grow up" and admit they existed in a cold, impersonal universe. He called religion a "neurosis," an "illusion," a "poison," and an "intoxicant." He pontificated, "But surely infantilism is destined to be surmounted. Men cannot remain children forever; they must in the end go out into 'hostile life.' We may call this 'education to reality.'"

One wonders where Freud went for his data. Did his theories tell us more about him and his difficult childhood than they did about the universe? Were the countless Christian martyrs who faced fire and sword for their faith in Christ-were they "weak individuals who could not face reality"? Did he ever enter a Christian church to discover people who were not weakened but empowered by the Gospel of Jesus?

Is a religion that commands us to give up our lives for one another a weak religion?

Fortunately, Freud was corrected by a later disciple, Eric Erickson, the neo-Freudian psychologist, who knew from experience that mature religion gives children a sense of trust, acceptance, love, and power.

Contrasting Nihilism With Faith

If we contrast nihilism, the philosophy of nothingness, with faith in God, we come up with the following picture:

Nihilism	Faith
Nothingness	A God who so loved the world that He gave His only Son for us.
Empty space within	"That you may be filled with all the fullness of God" (St. Paul).
Ultimately alone	God knows me and loves me
Life is meaningless	God wants me to behold His glory in heaven forever.
Pointless living	"For me to live is Christ" (St. Paul).
Hopelessness	Anticipation of a new heaven and a new earth.
Boredom	Enthusiasm.
Fear	Courage.
Worry	Peace.
Dullness	Zest for living.
Anxiety	Confidence.
No ultimate values	Responsibility and accountability to God.
Everything is relative	God is God. He is the Absolute.
No conscience	Sensitivity to right and wrong.

Other people get in	Other people are my brothers
the way	and sisters.
Scheme to outdo	Cooperate for the good of all.
others	
Gloom	Hunger for more life.
Despair	Hopefulness.
Potential suicide	Abundant life.
Feeling trapped in	Free to grow.
circle of existence	

Nihilism yields darkness, whereas the Christian Faith brings light.

The late Fr. Alexander Schmemann, of blessed memory, wrote,

> *I just finished "Gates of Eden" by Dickstein and thought that alongside popular courses like "Great Western Ideas" it would be useful to teach a course entitled "Great Western Errors," following approximately this plan: Rousseau and "Nature," with a capital N; the Enlightenment and "Reason," capital R; Hegel and "History," capital H; Marx and "Revolution," capital R; and finally, Freud and "Sex," capital S, realizing that the main error of each is precisely the capital letter, which transforms these words into an idol, into a false god that wreaks havoc on humanity.**

*The Journals of Father Alexander Schmemann, 1973-1983. Translated by Juliane Schmemann. SVS Press. Crestwood, NY 2000.

Postmodernists

Postmodernists (the politically correct) deny the existence of any universal objective reality. They believe that every cultural group has its own truth. They make up their own history, stating for example, that Plato was not Greek but a black from Africa, etc. Rationalism is replaced by irrationalism. Logic is replaced by the illogical; the real by the unreal and the true by the false.

It is reported that the first lunatic asylums appeared in Europe in 1533. George Bernard Shaw once said, "Earth is the planet to which all the other planets send their insane." I'm sure this may seem true at times.

But someone needs to keep reminding us of the great-truth that, "God so loved" this lunatic world that He gave His only begotten Son so that whoever believes in Him might be saved from lunacy and restored to sanity, saved from falsehood and restored to truth, saved from sin and restored to become a partaker of God's very nature.

The Plumb Line of Truth

People who say there is no right or wrong get into deep trouble when they begin comparing things and calling one thing better than another. For example, this happens when they begin condemning the atrocities of Hitler and Stalin and calling them inhuman and uncivilized. If they call this behavior wrong, then they are appealing to a definite standard of right and wrong.

C.S. Lewis described this when he wrote,

> The moment you say that one set of moral ideas can be better than another, you are, in fact, measuring them both by a standard, saying that one of them conforms to that standard more nearly than the other. But the standard that measures two things is something different from either. You are, in fact, comparing them both with some Real Morality, admitting that there is really such a thing as Right, independent of what people think, and that some people's ideas get nearer to that real Right than others. Or put it this way. If your moral ideas can be truer, and those of the Nazis less true, there must be something—some Real Morality— for them to be true about!*

So, if you're going to believe that there is no right or wrong, don't ever say that what Hitler or Stalin did was inhuman.

---

* *The Case for Christianity.* C.S. Lewis. The MacMillan Company, N.Y. 1947 pp. 11-12.

On September 11, 2001, Islamist fundamentalists, in a dastardly act of demonic violence, crashed planes into the World Trade Center and the Pentagon, killing thousands. This horrendous act blasted away the post-modernist argument that there is no absolute right or wrong.

If the post-modernist view is correct, then a monument should be erected to those terrorists, because, after all, they committed an "act of heroism" in sacrificing their lives for the "truth" they believed in.

It was not my truth: it was their truth. Yet all truth is equal, say the politically correct!

Another argument against those who say there is no right or wrong is the inner voice of conscience which accuses us when we do wrong and praises us when we do right.

Why should this voice exist?

Why does this divine umpire within us differentiate between right and wrong, calling the balls and strikes?

Does not this inner voice reveal to us that the God Who planted this voice within us differentiates between right and wrong, wants us to avoid evil and do that which is right and moral?

To quote C.S. Lewis again,

> The other bit of evidence is that Moral Law which He (God) has put into our minds. And this is a better bit of evidence than the other, because it is inside information. You find out more about God from the Moral Law than from the universe in general just as you find out more about a man by listening to his

conversation than by looking at a house he has built. Now, from this second bit of evidence we conclude that the Being behind the universe is intensely interested in right conduct—in fair play, unselfishness, and decency.*

Otherwise, He would not have given us a conscience.

C.S. Lewis continues,

My argument against God was that the universe seemed so cruel and unjust. But how had I got this idea of just and unjust? A man doesn't call a line crooked unless he has some idea of a straight line.**

The idea of a "straight line" has been planted in us by God Himself. It is part of the image of God in us and expresses itself through the voice of conscience. The "straight line" is the plumb line of God's Truth.

---

* *The Case for Christianity*. C.S. Lewis. The MacMillan Company, N.Y. 1947. p. 25.
** Ibid. p. 34

Everyone Believes

It is too simple to say that the problem for many people not accepting the truth is unbelief. Why? Because everyone believes. If you don't believe what is true, you will believe what is false.

Chesterton observed that the trouble with someone who does not believe in God is not that he will end up believing in nothing; it is, rather, that he will end up believing in anything and everything that comes along: the Jehovah's witnesses, the Moonies, David Koresh, etc.

"If (man's) craving for the mysterious, the wonderful, the supernatural, is not fed on true religion, it will feed itself on the garbage of any superstition that is offered to it," said George Tyrrell.

Everyone believes. If you don't believe what is true, you will believe what is false.

New Age

The most common heresy today is New Age, which is a grand collection of all the heresies (false teachings) that ever existed from the very beginning of time. All of these are now under one umbrella.

Go into any large bookstore, as I have, and expect to find ten or more bookstalls under "New Age" and only two or three under "Christianity" and "World Religions."

In what is considered a magnificently scientific age, in a society that is genuinely materialistic, the fastest growing religion (New Age) is built on pure fantasy.

If you don't believe in the one true God, you will end up, for example, believing in aromatherapy, which is the belief that breathing in certain aromas can bring inner peace and even cure cancer.

A bookstore in New York City is filled with books on magic and astrology. A salesperson said, "These are the kinds of books people want."

Does not this remind one of what Jesus said, "If the light in you is darkness, how great the darkness" (Matt. 6:23).

The follower of Christ is not so credulous as to accept New Age fantasizing without asking, "Is it true?" In this spurning of the truth of God for neo-pagan myths and fables, we are seeing the fulfillment of St. Paul's prophecy: "For the time will come," Saint Paul foresaw, "when they will not endure sound doctrine, but according to their own desires, because they have itching ears, they will heap up for themselves teachers; and they will turn their ears away from the truth, and be turned aside to fables" (2 Timothy 4:3-4).

The truth of Christ is the best defense against cults, myths and fables.

Spinning a Crystal

An example of this is a bishop who visited a well-educated couple. As they talked before lunch, the husband told the bishop that they just could not believe in the Virgin Birth of Jesus and the Resurrection. They thought Christianity was absurd. Then the wife called from the kitchen, "Honey, spin the crystal." The husband spun a multi-faceted crystal hanging from the chandelier above the dining room table. He kept looking into it until it stopped spinning. Then, he called to his wife, "It's okay," whereupon she brought in the dinner.

When the bishop asked about the crystal, he was told that it was their "spiritual experience," like a prayer which put them in touch with the universe. When the bishop asked if it ever said no, they replied, "never." When they went back to discussing Christianity, the couple repeated that they could not believe anything as absurd as the Virgin Birth and the Resurrection. At this point the bishop said, "But you believe in spinning a crystal?"

Truth: A Casualty

Truth is a casualty today. In public schools students are taught to "construct" their own truths and values. In some so-called Christian churches, students are even invited to write their own creed. Teachers are trained not to offer any direction, lest they hamper a child's "autonomy."

What is meaningful and what is not meaningful to me has displaced what is objectively true and what is objectively false. This means that there is no objective, absolute, transcendent truth. What is true or false, right or wrong, now resides not in God but in each individual. If it is meaningful to me, it is true and right. If it is not meaningful to me, it is not true and false. God has been dethroned along with His Truth with a capital "T".

St. Paul described the post-modernist situation when he wrote in 2 Thess. 2:11-12, "Therefore God sends upon them a strong delusion, to make them believe what is false, so that all may be condemned who did not believe the truth but had pleasure in unrighteousness."

In Romans 1:25 St. Paul says, "...they exchanged the truth of God for a lie..."

The individual now sits on God's throne, pontificating on everything.

Postmodernism (redefining truth according to one's whims) is not new. Already three thousand years ago in Israel there was a period when there was no ruling authority and "every man did what was right in his own eyes" (Judges 17:6).

How terribly deforming it is to believe that there is no objective truth outside oneself. As someone said, "You have to be sick to say no to truth."

Ten Commandments Obsolete

Another contemporary example of exchanging truth for a lie is the influential Ted Turner of CNN fame, who has declared the Ten Commandments "obsolete." He told members of the National Newspaper Association, "I bet nobody here even pays attention to 'em, because they are too old. When Moses went up on the mountain," said Turner, "there were no nuclear weapons, there was no poverty. Today, the Ten Commandments wouldn't go over. Nobody likes to be commanded. Commandments are out."

Actually, Turner has a few commandments of his own (ten to be exact) but he calls them "the ten voluntary initiatives." Truth no longer resides in God but in the individual who is now free to construct his own "voluntary initiatives."

It's interesting that when God drafted the Ten Commandments, He did not conduct a market survey to see what the people wanted. He drafted the Ten Commandments, and gave them to us written not on tissue paper but on stone tablets—never to be tampered with or revised.

Ted Koppel at Duke University

Speaking at Duke University Ted Koppel said,

We have actually convinced ourselves that slogans will save us. Shoot up if you must, but use a clean needle. Enjoy sex whenever with whomever you wish, but wear a condom. No! The answer is no. Not because it isn't cool or smart or because you might end up in jail or dying in an AIDS ward, but no because it's wrong, no because we have spent 5,000 years as a race of rational human beings, trying to drag ourselves out of the primeval slime by searching for absolutes. In its purest form, truth is not a polite tap on the shoulder. It is a howling reproach. What Moses brought down from Mount Sinai were not Ten Suggestions.

Science, Scientism and Truth

We owe much to science and respect it greatly for what it has accomplished. Behind every door of science that we open, whether it be biology, geology, entomology or zoology, we meet God at work. We discover the wondrous ways by which He has been, and is still working in the universe. We follow the traces of His footprints everywhere.

We respect science, but there is a certain philosophy of science called *scientism* that goes beyond the findings of science. It assumes that the scientific method is the only reliable road to truth and that the things science deals with are the most fundamental things that exist.

The trouble with scientism is that it denies a basic premise of true science, i.e., the true scientist is open to all evidence, from whatever quarter, whereas the believer in scientism has his mind made up in advance. Even before careful examination, the believer in scientism claims to know what is true and not true. He very unscientifically and arbitrarily closes the door of truth from any other source than science.

G.K. Chesterton, for example, contrasts those who believe in miracles with those who believe in scientism He writes, "The believers in miracles accept them (rightly or wrongly) because they have evidence for them. The disbelievers in miracles deny them (rightly or wrongly) because they have a doctrine against them."

Different Instruments for Each Science

In the search for truth one uses different instruments of investigation.

Every department of science has its own specific instruments for investigating truth: i.e., medicine—the scalpel; astronomy—the telescope; biology—the microscope; chemistry—the test tube, etc.

So it is with God. Because He is not physical and cannot be dissected with a scalpel or placed in a test tube, we use other instruments to investigate the truth about God, i.e., prayer , repentance, commitment, the Bible, the Church, divine revelation, purity of heart, etc.

Spiritual Tools for Spiritual Truths

When someone says, "Prove God to me and I will believe," we ask, "What do you mean by proof? Do you mean logical proof? Is God a geometric theorem to be proved logically? Do you mean scientific proof? Is God a material substance we can place in a test tube and analyze? There are different kinds of proofs for different things."

As George Buttrick said, "There is one kind of proof for potatoes, another for poems, another for persons, another for God."

The proof of God is to discover Him for yourself, not through logic or science but by faith, by surrendering your life to Him, by prayer, by repentance, through the Bible, the Church and the Sacraments. These are the tools we use to discover God Who is Spirit and Truth We use spiritual tools to discover spiritual truths.

Faith in God is never irrational, never against reason; it is beyond reason; therefore beyond logic and it is beyond scientific demonstration. After all, if we could analyze God in a test tube and understand him logically, He would not be God. We would be God. He would be less than we are. We would be greater.

Spiritual truths are discovered through spiritual tools.

Science is Not the Only Way to Truth

A braham Heschel wrote, "Science is not the only way to truth, and its methods do not represent all of human thinking. Indeed, they are out of place in that dimension of human existence in which God is a burning issue. God is not a scientific problem, and scientific methods are not capable of solving it… The moment we utter the name of God, we leave the level of scientific thinking and enter the realm of the ineffable."*

---

* *God in Search of Man*. Abraham Heschel. Farrar, Straus and Giroux. N.Y. 1955. p. 102

Science is Impossible Without Faith

Louis Cassels wrote in his book The Reality of God:

Every age has its superstitions, and ours is the notion that science is an infallible guide to truth. The corollary is that the only kind of reality worth bothering about is that which can be verified by the methods of physical science.

Scientists, if consulted, would vigorously refute this idea. They are keenly aware that science itself depends on assumptions—such as the order and intelligibility of the natural universe—which cannot be verified by scientific methods but must be accepted, so to speak, on faith. "Science is impossible without faith—the faith that nature is subject to law," says Norbert Wiener, the father of cybernetics.*

Since scientism closes off God and divine revelation, it leads to a bleak and chilling world view that considers the universe as impersonal and without purpose.

This was expressed by the poet T.S. Eliot when he wrote,

Endless invention, endless experiment,

Brings knowledge of motion, but not of stillness;

Knowledge of speech, but not of silence;

All our knowledge brings us nearer to our ignorance.

---

* *The Reality of God.* Louis Cassels. Herald Press. Scottdale, P.A. 1972. p. 15

All our ignorance brings us nearer to our death.

But nearness to death no nearer to God.

Where is the Life we have lost in living?

Where is the wisdom we have lost in knowledge?

Where is the knowledge we have lost in information?

Theodore Parker (19th century) wrote about the true purpose of science, "Every rose is an autograph from the hand of God...He has inscribed His thoughts in these marvelous hieroglyphics which sense and science have, these many thousand years, been seeking to understand."

A Christian Legacy

Someone said, "Science books are letters from God, telling how He runs the universe." Let us remember that without Christianity we wouldn't even have science.

Most of the early scientists were Christians: Copernicus, Kepler, Galileo, Newton, Pascal. They believed the world had an orderly structure that could be scientifically studied because it was created by an orderly God.

In Christianity, nature was no longer an object of worship as it was in pagan religions. Only then could it become an object of scientific study. Science, then, is one of the legacies of Christianity to the world.

The Limit to Science

Yet science is not without limitations. Archimandrite Sophrony tells the following story about the limits of science in discovering truth.

"I once heard the following story of a professor of astronomy who was enthusiastically discoursing in a planetarium on the nebulae and like marvels. Noticing an unpretentious priest who had joined his group of students, the professor asked him: 'What do your Scriptures say about cosmic space and its myriad stars?'

Instead of giving a direct answer the priest in turn posed a question. 'Tell me, Professor,' he said, 'do you think that science will invent still more powerful telescopes to see even farther into the firmament?' 'Of course, progress is possible and science will always be perfecting apparatus for exploring outer space,' replied the astronomer. 'There is hope, then, that one day you will have telescopes that can show all there is in the cosmos, down to the last detail?' 'That would be impossible—the cosmos is infinite,' replied the scientist. 'So there is a limit to science?' 'Yes, in that sense, there is.' 'Well, Professor,' said the priest, 'where your science comes to a full stop, ours begins, and that is what our Scriptures tell of.'"*

---

* *His Life is Mine.* Sophrony. SVS Press. Crestwood, N.Y. 1977. pp.56-57.

So, to scientism, which believes there is no truth beyond what science can give us, we say, NO! But to true science, we say YES!

True science continues to uncover truths about God's creation and leads to a greater appreciation of His wisdom and power. True science, like true theology, leads to doxology and praise to God as it uncovers untold marvels in the universe.

Two Men Look at the Universe

I share with you the views of two people who look at the universe to find the truth behind it: one a non-believer, the other a believer.

The non-believer is the famous astronomer, Carl Sagan, who spent much of his life gazing at the stars and galaxies and thinking about the place we humans occupy in this vast universe. This is what he said about it all:

> As long as there have been humans, we have searched for our place in the cosmos. Where are we? Who are we? We find that we live on an insignificant planet of a humdrum star lost in a galaxy tucked away in some forgotten corner of a universe in which there are far more galaxies than people.

Now doesn't that sound depressing? Sagan uses words such as "insignificant", "lost", "humdrum", and "forgotten!" What is the source of Carl Sagan's gloomy view of human life? Is it not his belief in scientism, i.e., that there is no truth beyond what science can give us, that there is no God, that there is only the cosmos in which everything is measured in light years and is counted in billions and trillions, in contrast to which we puny human beings hardly count for much?

When a scientist who was a believer encountered him one day, Dr. Sagan said to him, "I cannot understand why, with all your knowledge, you actually believe in God."

The believing scientist responded, "I cannot understand why you, Carl, with all your knowledge, do not believe in God."

The Prophet David

L et us look now at another person—a believer—who looked at the same universe Dr. Sagan studied, but drew a totally different conclusion.

This person is the Prophet David who looked not just at the universe but beyond the universe to see the infinite God Who exists above and beyond the cosmos. David believed that "in the beginning God created the heavens and the earth" (Gen. 1:1), and that God's highest act was to make us "in His own image."

We are certainly not great or powerful, but the magnificent Creator chose to make us in His image and likeness, and crowned us—small though we are—"with glory and honor."

David expressed this beautifully in Psalm 8:

Lord, our Lord, how majestic is your name in all the earth! You have set your glory above the heavens. When I consider your heavens, the work of your fingers, the moon and the stars, which you have set in place, what is man that you are mindful of him, the son of man that you care for him? You made him a little lower than the heavenly beings and crowned him with glory and honor. You made him ruler over the works of your hands; you put everything under his feet: all flocks and herds, and the beasts of the field, the birds of the air, and the fish of the sea, all that swim the paths of the seas.

Lord, our Lord, how majestic is your name in all the earth!" (Psalm 8:1-9).

Sagan looked at the universe and called man "puny". David looked at the same cosmos and asked God, "What is man that You are so mindful of him? You have made him a little lower than the heavenly beings."

Sagan, of course, is not typical of all astronomers. One astronomer who is a true scientist, and not a believer in scientism, said that every time he looks at the heavens through a telescope, he gets the feeling that Someone from up there is looking back at him; Someone Who created and sustains all that precise order in the universe; Someone Who so loved you and me that He gave His only begotten Son, so that all who believe in Him might not perish but have life everlasting" (John 3:16). And that is the truth above all truths; the Truth that redeems, saves, and sets us free.

Truth is "Invented"

We have now come to the point where truth is something to be invented rather than pursued.

A professor proclaimed in class one day that there is no absolute truth. This led a very sensible student to ask him, "Is that statement true?"

David Remnick points out in his book *Lenin's Tomb* that it was the return to history, the return to truth about the past, that was the beginning of the end for the Soviet Union. Solzhenitsyn, for example, believed that he had a God-given mission to tell the truth about the atrocities that atheism had wrought in our world, especially upon his fellow kulaks in the gulags. He placed the number of deaths at Soviet hands "at the lowest estimates, almost 60 million." This has to be the greatest holocaust of all times. In revealing the truth about these atrocities Solzhenitsyn was fundamentally a moral writer with spiritual impulses shaped by his Christian faith.

"The truth will set you free," said Jesus.

Ultimately, the truth as exposed by Solzhenitsyn did free the Soviet Union from communism.

Freedom: Grounded in Truth

True freedom is grounded in truth. Freedom by itself is not enough. Freedom standing by itself inevitably degenerates into license. Authentic freedom cannot exist without truth. Not my truth, your truth or her truth; not the truth of a class or a tribe or a nation, but God's TRUTH, with a capital "T", as in absolute Truth.

A few years ago, while visiting Mammoth Cave in Kentucky, I learned that spelunkers, before exploring unknown caverns, tie one end of a rope to a solid object outside the cave. As they grope their way through the maze of passageways, they slowly unwind the rope. Thus, if they get lost, they can easily find their way out by slowly re-winding the rope.

Similarly, we today need to be tied to some real answers, some basic certainties, some solid rock, some absolute truth, on which to stake our lives in this dark cavernous world. That unchanging certainty—that solid rock—is the Son of God, the Lord Jesus, "the Way, the Truth and the Life," Who is "the same yesterday, today, and forever."

"Heaven and earth will pass away, but my words will never pass away," said Jesus (Matt. 24:35).

T.S. Eliot asked, "Where is the wisdom we have lost in knowledge? Where is the knowledge we have lost in information?"

The answer for Orthodox Christians is the Lord Jesus, Son of God and Son of Man, "the Way, the Truth and the Life;" Jesus "the power of God and the wisdom of God" (St. Paul). The Truth of Christ is our lodestar.

Detecting the Counterfeit

Aperson who was sitting next to the chief of the counterfeit money section of Scotland Yard said to him, "I suppose you study a lot of counterfeit bills."

"No," he replied, "I study only genuine bills. The more I look at the genuine bills, the better I am able to detect what is counterfeit."

Is it not the same with us? The more we focus our attention on the Truth—Jesus—the better we are able to discern the counterfeits in life.

I once saw the following words on a bumper sticker, "Fight truth decay, read the Bible everyday." Just as counterfeit money presupposes the existence of good money, so counterfeit truths presuppose the existence of genuine Truth. Just as disorder presupposes order, blindness presupposes sight, and evil presupposes a standard of goodness, so the notion of error presupposes the existence of truth.

Such a standard of truth and goodness exists:

> "For the law was given through Moses; grace and truth came through Jesus Christ" (John 1:17).

> "For this I was born, and for this I have come into the world, to bear witness to the truth. Everyone who is of the truth hears my voice" (John 18:37), said Jesus.

Sanitizing History

George Orwell said once, "Any attack... on the concept of objective truth threatens in the long run every department of thought." This has now happened through postmodernism, the politically correct movement.

It has happened in public school textbooks that religiously avoid religion. For example, we know that the Bible was the engine that drove Martin Luther King, Jr. in the civil rights movement. Yet, this fact is omitted from school textbooks, thus imparting an incomplete education about King, whose great speeches are grounded in scriptural imagery and metaphors. Such textbooks will mention that he was influenced by Ghandi with no mention at all of the Bible. This is an example of how the postmodernists have distorted truth.

History is now whatever one wants it to be. Just change the facts to suit your taste, or rather your prejudice, and you come out with a do-it-yourself history. Take away a sense of history, and you destroy the Christian faith, which is based on historical fact:

> "In those days a decree went out from Caesar Augustus that all the world should be enrolled... when Quirinius was governor of Syria."

When Quirinius was governor of Syria. It's all history. It's geography, too.

When one visits the Holy Land, one combines history with geography and comes away with a rejuvenated faith. The truth of Christianity is not a myth or a legend; it is based on historical fact.

How Darwinism Distorts the Truth About God and Creation

L et us examine for a moment how the truth of God as Creator has been distorted.

The adherents of Charles Darwin have deified what they call evolution by natural selection. Natural selection which is the real core of Darwinism, is a blind process that evolves new forms of life by chance. Natural selection (blind chance) replaces God as Creator. Natural selection assumes that life is a product of forces that are impersonal and purposeless—that life is a cosmic accident. The fact that there is design in the universe is ruled out entirely, a priory. It is not even allowed into the discussion by Darwinists.

Yet the fact remains there is design in the universe. For example, speaking of the intricacy of DNA, Bill Gates said, "DNA is like a computer program, but far, far, more advanced than any software we have ever developed."

Does intelligent design come from non-design, from chance?

During the last half of the 20th century, advances in molecular biology and biochemistry have revolutionized our understanding of the miniature world within the tiny cell. Research has revealed that cells—the fundamental units of life—store, transmit, and edit information and use that information to regulate their most fundamental metabolic processes.

Far from characterizing cells as simple homogeneous globules of plasm, biologists now classify cells as, among other things, "distributive real time computers" or complex information processing systems.

The fantastic complexities within the microcosm of the cell beg for some kind of explanation. And the logical explanation is that design is the product not of blind chance but of a Master Designer.

One scientist wrote, "Einstein said, 'God does not play dice with the universe.' He was right. God plays scrabble" (Philip Gold).

That's why some two centuries ago, the English clergyman William Paley could illustrate the existence of design in the universe with this example:

> "Suppose you find a watch on the beach; would you assume it was the product of the wind or the waves? Of course not; and since living things exhibit the same structure, they too must be products of an intelligent agent."

Richard Dawkins, an atheist who is a zoologist, claims, "The universe we observe has precisely the properties we should expect if there is at bottom no design, no purpose, no evil, no good, nothing but pointless indifference."

Such assertions clearly go well beyond the domain of science in general, especially zoology.

Zoologists like Dawkins, should stick to zoology and not venture outside their field and make pronouncements on the origins of the universe.

But, because science has considerable authority in our culture, scientists are accorded great respect even when they step out of their own field of study and begin to dispense bad philosophy.

The eminent Roman Catholic theologian Cardinal Joseph Ratzinger wrote, "We must have the audacity to say that the great projects of the living creation are not the products of chance and error...They point to a creating Reason and show us a creating Intelligence, and they do so more luminously and radiantly today than ever before."

A revolution is taking place all around us today. Scientists are discovering massive evidence of design in DNA, in microscopic cells, etc. Nature herself, even in her fallen state, remains an icon of the glory of God.

One scientist said, "I am a scientist by training and I do not have sufficient faith to be an atheist, so I see no other choice." He continues, "To study the human nervous system, as I do, is to peer into the makeup of man who is made in God's image—to look at something fearfully and wonderfully made."

It takes greater faith to be an atheist than to believe in the Intelligent Master Designer who is the Lord Jesus Christ, Who not only made man but became man; Whose face was "full of grace and truth," and Who, when He appeared in Bethlehem as a defenseless, innocent Child, was saluted by the angelic hosts as they sang, "Glory to God in the highest!"

He is the Intelligent Master Designer of the Universe
Whom the Apostle John describes, "In the beginning
was the Word, and the Word was with God and the
Word was God. He was with God in the beginning.
Through Him all things were made; without Him noth-
ing was made that has been made" (John 1:3).

C.S. Lewis' Argument

To be an atheist one must believe that design in the universe comes not from an Intelligent Designer but from non-design, from blind chance.

Few people have expressed the fallacy of such thinking more potently than C.S. Lewis:

> *There are all sorts of different reasons for believing in God, and here I'll mention only one. It is this. Supposing there was no intelligence behind the universe, no creative mind. In that case nobody designed my brain for the purpose of thinking. It is merely that when the atoms inside my skull happen for physical and chemical reasons to arrange themselves in a certain way, this gives me a bye-product, the sensation I call thought. But if so, how can I trust my own thinking to be true? It's like upsetting a milk-jug and hoping that the way the splash arranges itself will give you a map of London. But if I can't trust my own thinking, of course I can't trust the arguments leading to atheism, and therefore I have no reason to be an atheist, or anything else. Unless I believe in God, I can't believe in thought: so I can never use thought to disbelieve in God.* *

---

* *The Case for Christianity.* C.S. Lewis. The MacMillan Co. p.32

The Jesus Seminar

An example of professional truth slayers today are those who reject the Bible's portrait of Jesus and try to come up with "the real Jesus," Whom they call the "historical Jesus."

You may have heard of the Jesus Seminar, where certain ultra liberal scholars get together and decide which words attributed to Jesus in the gospels are words that Jesus actually said.

Using color-coding and other media-friendly gimmicks, these self-proclaimed experts mark what Jesus could not possibly have said, what he probably didn't say, what he perhaps could have said, and what he probably did say The result is that, according to these "experts," Jesus didn't say most of what the gospels claim he said.

Isn't it amazing that so-called "scholars" 2,000 years later know the "historical Jesus" better than those who actually saw Him and heard and touched him! And wrote about Him! These so-called "experts" think they know better than the Church herself, which was there at the time and guarantees the truth of the Scriptures.

Even more amazing is that the "Jesus" produced by the Jesus Seminar sounds and acts just the way skeptical twentieth-century scholars would want him to. It is noteworthy that the Jesus Seminar does not include some of the major Biblical scholars of our day, but is made up of a tiny group of like-minded super liberals who disagree among themselves. Members of the seminar themselves come up with different pictures of Jesus. John Domenic Crossan sees Jesus as a Jewish peasant while Marcus Borg sees him as New Age guru. Yet as one scholar said, "the press eagerly publishes 'the latest conclusions of the Jesus Seminar' as if they represented the cutting edge of biblical scholarship."

The Jesus Seminar tells us more about the members of the seminar than it tells us about Jesus.

Skeptics have been denying Jesus' words for centuries, and their denial is based more on their own biases than on real evidence. It is based on their opinion of what Jesus could have said and done if He was just human.

We need to be careful when we hear the name "Jesus". It may not be the same Jesus Orthodox Christians believe in.

How true are the words of St. Augustine who said, "If you believe in the gospel only what you like, and reject what you don't like, it is not the gospel you believe, but yourself." This is what has happened to the gospel at the hands of the Jesus Seminar. It's not a new search for truth. It's dogmatic disbelief disguised as scholarship.

The Name "Jesus"

As already stated, the name "Jesus" has been emptied by many of its true meaning. Yet no name is more precious to Orthodox Christians than the name "Jesus!"

Who is this Jesus? Is He just man? Is He just God? Is He both God and man? Is He the greatest teacher who ever lived? Exactly who is this Jesus?

According to Orthodox teaching, Jesus is Lord, the eternal Son of God, the Alpha and the Omega, the Beginning and the End, the Second Person of the Holy Trinity. "He was in the beginning with God; all things were made through him, and without him was not anything made that was made. In Him was life, and the life was the light of men. The light shines in the darkness, and the darkness has not overcome it" (John 1:2-4).

Jesus is not just God. He is not just man. He is both God and man in one and the same Person, God in human flesh; God coming close to us to love us, to embrace us, to save us, to lift us to heaven, to make us partakers of divine nature. Truly, there is no other name under heaven given among mortals by which we must be saved. For "at the name of Jesus every knee shall bow in heaven, and on earth, and under the earth" (Philippians 2:10). He is the Truth Who saves, sanctifies, and sets us free.

The "Sanitized" Jesus

I say this because we live in a day when Jesus is being "sanitized." Many so-called Christian "churches" have adopted a politically correct Jesus who is anything you want Him to be.

In an age of pluralism, the last thing the politically correct people want is to present a Jesus who said, "I am the way, the truth, and the life. No man comes to the Father except through me."

In fact, one so-called "Christian" said at a supposedly Christian conference,

> I grew up in a time and place where it was taken for granted that Christianity was the only true religion and Jesus the only way of salvation. That's why we had missionaries…I find it literally incredible to think that the God of the whole universe has chosen to be known in only one religious tradition, which just fortunately happens to be of our own.

What this person needs to know that non-Christian religions are also exclusivistic. They tolerate no deviation from the truths they teach. In fact, some of them will kill an adherent who chooses to convert.

The Apostolic Faith
in Jesus

The Orthodox Church upholds the apostolic faith concerning Jesus. It is the Jesus Whom the apostles made known and handed down to us, not as each individual would like Him to be, or imagines Him to be.

It is not the Jesus Seminar, politically correct Jesus, but the Jesus who is "the same yesterday, today, and forever."

Jesus Himself warned us about this when He said that in the last times "false Christs and false prophets will arise and show great signs and wonders, so as to lead astray, if possible, even the elect" (Matthew 24:24. See also Mark 13:22).

Truth is not an abstract code. It is a Person, the Second Person of the Holy Trinity. To love truth is to love Jesus. To love Jesus is to love truth.

Fr. George Florovsky said that "truth is living and existential, an ever-challenging reality in the life of every Christian." If truth is "living" and "existential" and "ever-challenging" it is because Truth is not an abstract code, but a living Person, Who lives within the Church and within us and confronts us with the truth about ourselves, through the Bible and that inner voice called conscience.

Jesus is not abstract Truth but Personal Truth that saves as no other truth can save.

He—Jesus—is the "power of God unto salvation," wrote St. Paul.

He is the saving Truth of the Gospel. He is not the Truth of the past but also the Truth of the present and the truth of future, Who has His continuing presence in the life of the Church. He is the Truth "who was, and is, and is to come" (Rev. 4:8).

For Orthodox Christians Jesus is God the Son Who assumed flesh in Bethlehem, found a home in Nazareth, died on Golgotha, was raised after three days, ascended into heaven, and now sits at the right hand of God the Father where He intercedes in our behalf and waits to welcome us home when we pass from this life.

Orthodox Christians believe with St. Paul that "the truth is in Jesus" (Eph. 4:21); that Christ is "the wisdom of God and the power of God"; that He is the One by, in, and for Whom all things exist and subsist, Whom God has made head over all creation, and Who, now and for-ever, is truly "all and in all."

"He (Jesus) is the icon of the invisible God" (Col. 1:5).

"If we know the Son, we know the Father also" writes the Apostle John (Jn. 8:19).

He is the One Whom we confess along with St. Peter, "Thou art the Christ, the Son of the living God!"

His is the One Whom we believe and confess to be the eternal Word of God, Who "became flesh and dwelt among us" and that "we have seen His glory, as of the only-begotten Son, in the bosom of the Father."

Jesus did not say, "You shall know a truth…" or just any truth. He spoke of knowing *the* truth. "I am the… Truth," He said. Truth is a Person, and that Person is the Son of the living God.

Appearing on the Dick Cavett show, the Archbishop of Canterbury said, "Jesus is the Son of God, you know." Jane Fonda, also on the same show, said, "Maybe He is for you, but He's not for me." The Archbishop responded, "Well, either He is or He isn't."

Someone once defined hell as "truth known too late".

Whatever Happened to Sin?

Another word that has been redefined today is the word "sin."

Dr. Karl Menninger, eminent psychiatrist, wrote a book a few years ago entitled *Whatever Became of Sin?* His main theme was that we have gotten smarter and have invented some new "respectable" words for some old and ugly ways of living: prostitutes are now called "escorts"; adultery is called an "affair" and is even considered a "means to personal fulfillment"; fornication is called "living together", etc. In other words, sin has been redefined in such a way that it no longer exists.

But it does exist and it creates hell in people. To alter the label on the bottle does not change the character of the contents. Poison is poison, give it whatever name you please.

One of the great tricks of Satan—the great deceiver—has always been: "Never call a sin by its right name. Call it by a nice, fair, innocent name."

We see this in the parable of the Prodigal Son. When he left home and was wasting his father's substance, he was merely "seeing the world." When he was bankrupt through riotous living, he probably called it "being a little wild." It was only when he landed in the barnyard with the pigs that he found the right name for his behavior. "I have sinned against heaven and before you," he said to his father. And that was the beginning of his salvation. He saw himself as he really was and called his behavior by its right name: sin.

The truth will make you free, but first it may make you miserable. Salvation will never come to us unless we first face our sin, call it by its right name, and surrender it to God. Sin is not the cold, impersonal breaking of a commandment. All sin is sin against love. Our relationship to God is like the intimate relationship of husband and wife.

Sin: Infidelity to Love

A s such, sin is infidelity to love. When we sin, we break not just a commandment; we break God's heart, as the heart of one partner in marriage is broken when the other is unfaithful. Sin is personal unfaithfulness to Christ our Bridegroom. We need to look at the cross and say, "I caused that. My sin crucified Him." Without a strong sense of personal sin, there can be no guilt and no repentance.

Salvation for David began when he said, "Against Thee, Thee only have I sinned, O Lord, and done that which is evil in Thy sight." He called sin by its right name. He acknowledged and confessed the reality and truth of his condition. And that was the beginning of his salvation. He acknowledged and confessed the truth about himself.

The Word "God"

Another of our sacred words that is being emptied of its true meaning is the word God.

A student came to a pastor once and said, "I have decided that I cannot and do not believe in God." "All right," said the pastor. "But describe for me the God you don't believe in." The student proceeded to sketch his idea of God. When he finished, the pastor said, "Well, we're in the same boat. I don't believe in that kind of God either." His god was the opposite of Jesus.

How many different meanings people give to the word "God." People are experts at creating "gods". The word "god" can mean anything today. One must ask, "Which God? Whose God? What do you mean by God—your god or the real God?"

How many of us grow up with childish definitions of God that we never outgrow because we cease to grow spiritually. We go through life with a kindergarten concept of God. What do we mean when we say "God"? Are we talking about someone vague and abstract?

Absolutely not! We mean Someone very specific. We mean a real historical Person, Jesus. "No one has ever seen God; the only Son, who is in the bosom of the Father, he has made Him known" (John 1:18).

Jesus, who is "in the bosom of the Father," i.e., in the closest possible relationship to Him, only He can show us who the Father is. And indeed He does!

Jesus says, "He who sees me sees the Father... I and the Father are one." We look through Jesus as through a window to see God the Father. This is especially so with the Pantocrator icon of Jesus which looks down at us from the domes of Orthodox churches. We look through the figure of the Pantocrator Jesus to see the Father. The Father is like Jesus. Only through Jesus can we see the Father.

Apart from Jesus, the Father remains unknown, an abstraction. So, by "God" we mean Jesus, but we mean more than Jesus. We mean also the Father and the Holy Spirit. The only way we Orthodox Christians can express everything we mean by that overwhelming word "God" is to say, "Father, Son and Holy Spirit." The Father Who loves me. The Son Who redeems me. The Holy Spirit Who dwells in me and empowers me.

As Saint Theophan the Recluse said, "We are saved by the good will of the Father, through the merits of the Son, by the grace of the Holy Spirit."

We need to fill the word "God" with all its true and sacred meaning as we do in that great doxological prayer:

> "Glory to the holy, consubstantial, life-creating, and undivided Trinity, the Father, the Son, and the Holy Spirit, now and ever and unto the ages of ages. Amen."

That is the One, True God who revealed Himself in the Lord Jesus.

The Word "Happiness"

Another word that has been emptied of truth is the word happiness.

What is happiness? Happiness is not money. It is not sex. Happiness is not drugs. It is not alcohol. It is not a Caribbean cruise. It is not power or popularity. If the road to hell is paved with good intentions, the road to happiness is paved with countless false and misleading signposts or definitions.

There is only one way to happiness for the Christian, i.e., to know, love, and serve the one true God, Father, Son and Holy Spirit. Happiness is God. Happiness is knowing that you are loved by God.

As one Christian confessed, "When I look back upon the years of my own life, I see quite clearly that I owe my present inner happiness, my peace, my confidence and my joy essentially to one fact: I am certain that I am infinitely and personally loved by God."

That is the true Christian definition of happiness: to live for God in Christ and to know that you are infinitely and personally loved by God and that nothing in all creation—not even death—will ever be able to separate you from the love of God in Christ Jesus. That is true happiness.

Love

Another sacred word that has been emptied of truth and polluted with false meanings today is the word love.

True love, agape, means to care deeply, to serve, to give one's life, if need be, for the one loved. The great example of this is God who "so loved the world that he gave his only Son..."

Love today means anything but giving. In fact, it has come to mean not giving, but taking. Love is not agape anymore; it is lust. It is manipulating or using the other person for one's selfish gratification or profit. It treats people as disposable pieces of Kleenex. It has done away with that deep giving of oneself called commitment in favor of just "living together" not "until death do us part," but until some other "meaningful relationship" comes along.

Once God is removed from life, words such as love lose their meaning. For how can we know what true love is without God who alone is love? Without God sacred words such as love become polluted and identified with the sewer experiences of life. It is only in Christ that words—and life itself—are redeemed and find their true meaning.

The Word "Sex"

Another word that has been denuded of truth and lost its meaning today is the word sex. It is a word that has all but been taken over by the devil. It has been polluted with every kind of uncleanness.

The Wall Street Journal reported some time ago that Helen Gurley Brown, retiring editor of Cosmopolitan magazine, created a world "where AIDS is never mentioned, where multiple sex partners are celebrated, and where multiple sex liaisons are dismissed as hanky-panky."

Yet the word "sex" does not belong to the devil or to Helen Gurley Brown, or to Kinsey. It belongs to God. He is the One who made it. After creating man and woman and ordering them to multiply, God not only said that sex was "good," as he had said of all his previous creations, He now said that it was "very good" (Genesis 1:31).

When God created sex, He said to Himself that he had created something very beautiful, very holy, truly worthy of Himself. He created it for a special relationship called marriage which He blessed then as He does now. And sex, like anything else, is fulfilling only when one follows the manufacturer's directions.

A Symbol of Total Giving

Sexual love is a symbol. It is a sign and seal of total commitment, of the total giving of one's self to the person loved, total sharing of all that we have and are, total faithfulness and total unity.

Sex is not just a physical act. It is a physical expression, but a physical expression of something that is deeply spiritual. It is an act that expresses the total giving of one's self to the one loved for all eternity. It is to love the other with all of one's mind, heart, soul, and strength. It is, in fact, the most beautiful icon on earth of God's love for us. It is an all-consuming love of agape, philia and eros.

If the physical act of love does not express this total giving of one's self to the one loved, then it is a lie. It is the prostitution of something that is sacred.

No relationship is ever "meaningful" if it does not express this kind of permanent commitment and love. This is why promiscuity breeds the death of love and can deprive sex of meaning in one's marriage. A love that is moved and guided by the love of God ought to be—and is— the most fulfilling and meaningful love in the world.

Sex can never be what it was created to be without God, never as fulfilling, never as meaningful, never as joyful, never as satisfying.

That is why marriage is a sacrament in the Orthodox Church: to enhance and make possible in Christ a true and lasting love that will be a symbol of total giving and a true icon on earth of God's love for us.

We need to reclaim the word "sex" for God by giving it its proper definition. It needs to be cleansed and given back to the Creator. It is His word—a sacred word—for a holy love and a sacred relationship: marriage.

This is God's truth about sex which the world is seeking to pollute and transform into a sewer word.

The Word "Church"

Another word that is being slaughtered today and needs to be defined properly is the word church. Look at the tremendous variety of groups that call themselves "churches" (25,000 of them at one estimate).

In fact, anyone can establish a "church." There are many cults and other groups today that use the word "church" very freely. But are they truly churches? Were they founded by Jesus and the apostles? Try to find a connection between the Christian Science Church or the Mormon Church and the early apostles. You never will! What kind of unbroken historical connection do these so-called "churches" have with the apostles and the early church?

If the devil appears as an angel of light and even quotes Scripture, then he can certainly use even "churches" to lead people away from the one true God and His plan of salvation.

We need to define our terms carefully. Exactly what do we mean when we say "church"? We Orthodox Christians mean by "church" the body through which Christ is present and active in the world today. It was founded by Christ through the apostles and has maintained a living, historical connection with the apostles through the ordination of its clergy. The bishop who ordains an Orthodox priest today can trace his ordination historically all the way back to the apostles, and through them to Christ. This is a guarantee that the Orthodox Church was not founded by someone called Joe Smith one hundred-and-fifty years ago, but by Christ Himself, and that it traces its existence historically back to Jesus. We call this "apostolic succession."

Apostolic Succession

The Church that has apostolic succession is the authentic and genuine Church or Body of Christ in the world today. It continues to teach not one man's interpretation or misinterpretation of the faith, but the complete deposit of faith as it was handed down to the apostles by Jesus.

A bumper sticker I once saw said, "Orthodoxy: telling the truth since 33A.D." It is the Church that gave us the Bible.

Thus, there are some very important questions to ask when one hears the word "church." Was this church founded by God or by man? Does it have an unbroken historical connection with the early Apostolic Church? How else can I be certain that what it teaches is truly apostolic, truly Christian, truly the word of God and not one man's interpretation or misinterpretation of that faith?

A church is the true Church of Christ if it can show historically that it was founded by Christ and has maintained a living connection over the centuries with that early Church of the Apostles.

We need this historical connection in order to be assured that the deposit of truth and faith has not been tampered with, but has been handed down to us in its entirety.

"We Have Found the True Faith"

Frederica Matthews-Green, a convert to the Orthodox Church, in her book *Facing East* is not antagonistic toward the Protestantism she left behind. She says that at the end of each divine liturgy, Orthodox Christians sing, "We have found the true faith, worshipping the undivided Trinity Who has saved us."

What does this mean? She says, "Our hymn doesn't say that nobody else has any truth at all, just that we're sure we do.

While we believe that Jesus is the only way to the Father and that the Orthodox Church today is the same Church He established, we don't presume God is unable to save people who follow Jesus in other churches.

But whatever truth there may be elsewhere, we assert confidently that we have found it fully here." *

* *Facing East.* Frederica Matthews-Green. Harper San Francisco 1997

Sacred Tradition

St. Irenaeus (130-200 AD) wrote, "Read the Holy Scriptures in the presence of a presbyter (priest) who has the apostolic tradition." The apostolic tradition is the deposit of faith entrusted to the apostles by the Lord Jesus.

Sacred Tradition includes the Bible, the writings of the Church Fathers, the decisions of the Ecumenical Councils, the Creed, the liturgies and other worship services of the Church. We need Sacred Tradition to safeguard the truth of Christ.

G.K. Chesterton defined Sacred Tradition as follows:

> Tradition means giving votes to the most obscure of all classes, our ancestors. It is the democracy of the dead. Tradition refuses to submit to the small and arrogant oligarchy of those who happen to be walking about.

We need the Apostolic Tradition in order to protect and better understand the Scriptures. "If there is no immune system to resist heresy, there will soon be nothing but the teeming infestation of heresy [false teaching]," said Dr. Thomas Oden.

What is this protective "immune system"? It is the Church with its Sacred Tradition.

Beware of anyone who says, "Sola Scriptura. The Bible alone." The Bible does not stand alone. Its proper setting is the Church which is its divinely appointed guardian and interpreter.

The original Apostolic Tradition, or deposit of faith, did not disappear through the ages. It survives in the Orthodox Church which is a living, historical continuation of the early Church of the apostles, "the pillar and foundation of truth" (I Tim 3:15).

Sacred Tradition is grounded in the Truth that has been deposited in the Church by Jesus from the very beginning and has been preserved in the Church by the Holy Spirit through the uninterrupted apostolic succession of the episcopal ministry.

The best definition of Sacred Tradition is that it is the life of the Holy Spirit in the Church through the centuries since Pentecost, guiding the Church to all truth.

Truth is thus safeguarded through the abiding presence of the Holy Spirit in the Church, the same Holy Spirit Who "spoke through the prophets" and guided the apostles, is still guiding the Church into a fuller understanding of Divine Truth from glory to glory.

This is the "immune system" which guards the truth from heresy.

If the Bible is read without the presence of "a presbyter who has the apostolic tradition," then some other person will step into the vacuum to create his own private "tradition" which will not be apostolic but the whim of one's fancy.

This is the reason there are so many different denominations, which call themselves "churches." Each one of these denominations reads the Scriptures but without the "apostolic tradition" which guides one to the proper, divinely revealed understanding of the Bible. Lacking the "apostolic tradition," these so-called "churches" establish a personal, individual tradition of their own that is not in agreement with the original catholic tradition of the apostles.

For example, the Mormons believe that the correct interpretation of the Bible is to be found in the Book of Mormon, allegedly revealed by an angel to Joseph Smith. The Book of Mormon replaces the Apostolic Tradition entrusted by Jesus to the apostles.

Some time ago I saw a paid TV ad by the Mormons. It showed two books: the Bible and the Book of Mormon. Slowly the Bible was panned out, only the Book of Mormon remained. And the announcer said, "What you really need to understand the Bible is the Book of Mormon. Write or call and we'll send you one today." And what does the Book of Mormon teach? It teaches that the entire New Testament is false. It brings in an entirely new revelation of God's truth that is totally fictional and man-made.

Mary Baker Eddy, founder of the Christian Science Church, teaches that the true understanding of the Bible is to be found in her book *The Key to the Understanding of Scriptures.* Her book replaces the entire Apostolic Tradition of the Church, distorting completely the truth of Christ.

The same happens with many of the Protestant denominations. The original "Apostolic Tradition" is replaced by some individual's personal and private understanding of what the Bible teaches. The result is that many of the core teachings of Jesus are misinterpreted or denied. Thus, the truth of Christ is distorted. Man-made traditions replace the divinely revealed "apostolic tradition," which abides in the Church and is none other than the presence of the Holy Spirit abiding in the Body of Christ, the Church, guiding it to all truth.

Thus, St. Irenaeus writes, "Read the Holy Scriptures, by all means, but always in the presence of a presbyter (who represents the Church) and has the apostolic tradition."

The Bible does not stand alone. It needs prayer. It needs the presbyter and the bishop. It needs the Church. It needs the Apostolic Tradition.

If Sacred Tradition is the Holy Spirit continuing to abide in the Church and guiding it to all truth, then Sacred Tradition is the guardian and keeper of truth.

There are so-called "Christian" churches today that deny the reality of Christ's Resurrection, condone abortion, doubt Jesus' miracles, question the divinity of Jesus, deny the Virgin Birth, and create liturgical blessings for same-sex unions.

This is a complete denial of the truth of the Bible and the Apostolic Tradition.

Pluriform Truths

The presiding bishop of one very liberal non-Orthodox church spoke often of "pluriform truths." According to such "pluriform truths," there is no transcendent truth.

One can hold directly contradictory truths as if they were all true.

There is pluriformity, i.e., only my truth and your truth and his truth and her truth; and even my truth is true only as long as I want it to be. In other words, I determine what God is and I determine what truth is.

If this same principle of "pluriform truths" were applied to science, the results would be catastrophic.

Yet, pluralism is dominant today. There is no absolute truth; there are only different points of view which one must accept without questioning.

A World War II pilot said once, "When I became a pilot, I had to learn the laws of aerodynamics. I went to a training school that was authorized to teach me. There I expected and found teachers to give me the facts, not their own personal opinions, not "pluriform truths," but the facts about the laws of aerodynamics."

If there are laws of aerodynamics, and physics, and astronomy and biology, which cannot be argued with, but only obeyed, why should we feel that there are "pluriform truths" when it comes to God's truth and

God's moral laws? If God exists and has spoken to us in Christ, then what He says to us should be even more true than the laws of aerodynamics.

Yet, there are so-called Christian Churches today that deny this reality.

Discovering that her son and his girlfriend were living together, one mother said to her Episcopalian friend, "They keep a book on their coffee table by your church's Bishop Jack Spong—saying unmarried sex is okay, as long as it is monogamous."

There are "churches" that say, "you're gay? use drugs? believe in goddess worship? are a radical feminist? Come on in! We're so broad that we welcome everyone!"

One cannot say that and believe that one is a true believing Orthodox Christian.

These are norms. There are standards. There is Truth with a capital T.

Tolerance: An Overrated Virtue

Without the parameters of the Bible and Sacred Tradition there are no goal posts, no boundaries to truth, no plumb line.

Tolerance has become the virtue of the day.

I agree with William F. Buckley Jr. when he says, "Tolerance is an overrated virtue." And I agree even more with G. K. Chesterton when he writes, "One's mind should not be so open that the brains fall out."

Too often we have applied tolerance where it does not belong. We have become tolerant about crime, tolerant about immorality, tolerant about violence, tolerant about truth, tolerant about right and wrong.

But science, for example, is not tolerant. It is highly intolerant. Water is always H2O. Mathematics is not tolerant. Two plus two always equals four—never four-and-a-half.

The airline pilot is not broad-minded and tolerant about the laws of aerodynamics. He is very narrow-minded, intolerant about those laws.

In the same way, Jesus was not tolerant toward selfishness but highly intolerant. He was not tolerant toward sin, but highly intolerant, "Enter by the narrow gate," He said, "for wide is the gate and broad is the way that leads to destruction, and there are many who go in by it. Because narrow is the gate and difficult is the way which leads to life, and there are few who find it" (Matt. 7:13-14).

The early Christians were highly intolerant of heresy and false teaching. Polycarp, for example, tells the story of the Apostle John going to bathe in Ephesus. When he learned that the heretic Cerinthus was in the bathhouse, John ran out exclaiming, "Let us fly, lest even the bath-house fall down, because Cerinthus, the enemy of the truth, is within." Cerinthus, a Gnostic, denied the very humanity of Jesus together with His sacrifice on the cross and resurrection. He had been expelled from the Church for his heretical ideas. The Apostle John wanted everyone to know the real Jesus and not be fooled by fakes and frauds, some of whom were very slick. If Jesus is the only way to the Father and to salvation, if He is the Way, the Truth and the Life, that truth had to be protected. The early Christians were very uncompromising when it came to protecting the truth of Christ.

Orthodoxy believes that God's truth needs the presbyter, the bishop, and the Church. It needs the Apostolic Tradition. Otherwise truth becomes the whim of everyone's fancy.

Orthodoxy whose aim is to preserve the true faith and the true worship of God is faced today with perhaps its greatest challenge ever.

"Bad philosophy needs good philosophy," said C.S. Lewis.

So it is that today, "Bad theology needs good theology." We need not only to proclaim the truth but also to live it and to be able to give a reason for the faith that is in us.

Indeed we need to be possessed by the Truth.

St. Paul writes, "Stand, therefore, having girded your loins with truth" (Eph. 6:14). We do not stand but fall when we gird over our loins with untruth, lies, error, falsity.

St. Peter urges us to be prepared to defend truth, "Always be prepared to give an answer to everyone who asks you to give the reason for the hope you have, but do this in gentleness and respect..." (I Peter 3:15).

I best defend the Truth when I live it.

Abortion and Truth

A ll through the centuries, God's people have applied the teaching of the Bible to the matter of abortion and have denounced it in the strongest possible terms.

Michael Gorman researched the early church's attitude toward abortion, and what did he find? He says three main themes came up over and over:

1. the fetus is the creation of God;
2. abortion is murder; and
3. the judgment of God falls upon those guilty of abortion.

That's the Christian truth on abortion from the days of the apostles. Any other position is just not Christian.

Up until the past few decades, this was understood by all nations where the majority of people were Christian.

Would you believe that even Planned Parenthood once spoke out against abortion? A Planned Parenthood pamphlet from 1963 said, "An abortion kills the life of a baby after it has begun. It is dangerous to your life and health."

So, then, what changed? Planned Parenthood changed and public morality changed.

The truth, however, hasn't changed. God has not changed. Orthodox Christianity has not changed. The Bible's revelation that life is sacred from the womb to the grave has not changed.

The Relative and the Absolute

Recently I heard a Christian apologist argue that either Christianity was objectively true, accessible to anyone with rational sense, or it was a preposterous lie. "If I say it is raining today," said the apologist, "that is either true or not true. It can't be almost true, or figuratively true. It is objectively true.

Likewise, when I say, 'Jesus Christ rose from the dead,' it is either true or it is sheer fantasy." Jesus did not say, "I have come to start a discussion group about what is true." Rather, He came saying, "I am the Way, the Truth, and the Life."

We Orthodox need to proclaim boldly what Jesus said, "I am the Truth."

He did not say, "I am custom." Therefore custom should always yield to truth; tradition with a small "t" should always yield to Tradition with a capital "T".

For Truth is a Person. Truth is not sheer subjectivity.

The truth of Jesus is utterly inseparable from His life, death, and resurrection. In Christ, true man and true God, we discover the fullness of truth about God, about ourselves, and the purpose of our existence.

Yet, the world says, "Relativity is what we must live by now. Everything is relative."

Almost every student entering college today is taught that all truth is relative.

We ask: Relative? Relative to what? Everything has to be relative to something that is absolute. Nothing that is relative stands alone! Every branch belongs to a tree. Every truth is related to some absolute. The Absolute, of course, is God.

There is about us today what someone called an absolutophobia, an unwillingness to say that some behavior is just plain wrong.

"Do you believe in the Absolute?" a student once asked a professor. "No," said the professor. Then the student asked, "Is that an absolute statement?" Not all things are relative. Albert Einstein himself, who discovered the theory of relativity, said, "Philosophers play with the word relativity, like a child with a doll...It (relativity) does not mean that everything in life is relative."

There are absolutes. God's truth is absolute.

Moral Relativism

Moral relativists are those who do not believe in moral absolutes. They believe that there is no distinction between virtue and vice. But such thinking is untenable.

Who will concede that there is ultimately no significant moral difference between Hitler and Mother Teresa? Who is willing to believe that genocide, rape, and murder are just "cultural behaviors"? Why should the moral relativist complain if someone took a sledgehammer to his Rolls Royce? After all, for someone who says, "Your values are true for you, but not for me," there can be no objectively degrading actions.

Moral relativists condemn those who seek to impose their morality on others. Yet they themselves seek to impose their relativistic morality on others.

Do they believe that trying to rescue a drowning child and murdering that child are morally neutral? Do they think it was wrong for the Allied forces to "impose" their morality on Hitler, who invaded many militarily weaker countries and caused 30 million deaths in World War II?

Aren't you glad our government "imposes its morality" on rapists, murderers, thieves, and child molesters? If your sister or mother were being raped, would you stand by because you wouldn't want to impose your morality on the rapist?

Moral relativism cannot stand morally or logically.

Let us remember here that there is a difference between relativity and relativism. Relativity is a scientific concept. Relativism is a philosophical theory which hijacks science to try to prove that there is no absolute truth because everything—including God's laws—is relative. Relativism renounces logic by teaching that there is no absolute except the truth that there is no absolute truth.

S.M. Hutchens wrote, "A liberal wants truth, which includes the maxim that there is no truth."

All Truth is Relative to Jesus

In one sense, we Christians do believe that all truth is relative. All truth, all truthful living is relative to the life, death, and resurrection of Jesus. We really would have no idea of what is going on in the world, of how to think about things, if it were not for God's having loved us enough to send us His Son, who incarnates the truth, and the Spirit who guides us into all truth.

As Jesus said in John 16:13, "When the Spirit of truth comes, He will guide you into all truth." He will guide us, i.e., the Holy Spirit.

Truth, Christian truth, is not an achievement of man's thinking. It is a gift. It is grace. It is divine revelation. "The law was given by Moses. Grace and truth came through Jesus Christ" (John 1:17).

"Consecrate them in the truth; your word is truth," prayed Jesus in the Great Priestly Prayer. He was praying this prayer for His disciples and for us.

"One word of truth outweighs the whole world," says a Russian proverb.

A Bahai Teacher

A Bahai teacher was explaining that truth comes from many sources. He used the illustration of light coming in through many windows in a wall. "Jesus is just one window through which the light shines," he said. "Confucius is another window. Mohammed another window. Buddha still another window."

A Christian in the audience said to the Bahai teacher, "I beg to disagree. Jesus is not just another window. He is the light itself; He is the sun, that shines in through all the windows of the world."

"I am the light of the world," said Jesus, "whoever follows me shall not walk in darkness, but shall have the light of life." He is the light and whoever walks in His light walks in the truth and has the light of life.

There are many religions, but there is only one Gospel.

Distorting Sacred Words

We have already discussed that we need to be neptic or vigilant when it comes to the meaning of words. For example, many so-called Christian groups use the same words Orthodox Christians do, words such as Jesus, Savior, the Trinity, salvation, Church, but they have redefined, redesigned, and distorted these words to mean the opposite of what the Bible and the Church mean by them. The words are the same but the meaning is different.

There is no salvation, for example, in a Jesus who is the Son of Mary but not the eternal, pre-existing, ever-existing, only begotten Son of God.

What is more sacred to Orthodox Christians than the Eucharist? One will find the word "Eucharist" used in many, many churches. Yet many have distorted the basic meaning of what Communion is.

When Jesus said, "This is my body," He meant exactly what He said. He was giving us Himself. He did not say, "This bread represents my body...This wine symbolizes my blood." Yet the Eucharist today is not true Communion in many churches because some people have chosen to re-define the truth of God's word.

We do not manufacture our own definitions when it comes to God's truth. The Eucharist is not what we say it is; it is what God says it is.

The following story from the Desert Fathers shows how people often change God's truth in order to believe what they wish.

> *A young Abbot was counseled in this way by a Holy man: today many people, wishing for an excuse not to do what God asks of them, find fault with the teaching of the Holy Church and reject correct Christian belief. Instead, they choose to believe what they wish. This is akin to a man not wishing to believe that he will die, simply because the notion does not comfort him. Not only will he fail to prepare for death, as one ought to do, but he will inevitably find himself in the snare of death. Correct belief is not based on what we wish were true, but on truth itself!*

Why Are Religions Truths Disputed?

Why is it that scientific truths are accepted without argument, whereas religious truths are disputable?

Pascal offered the answer three centuries ago, He said, "If geometrical theorems also touched on human desires and passions, as the truths of faith do, then geometry would have given rise to as many objections as religion has."

Geometry remains external to life. Religious truths, on the other hand, affect life directly.

When one believes that God exists, that He will reward us for everything we have done in life, then we are obliged to change our lives to conform to God's will. Some people refuse to change their way of living. This gives rise to objections and disputes in religion which do not occur in science. Some people wish to follow their own desires and passions, so they seek to deny God's truth or change it. Often this leads to atheism or agnosticism.

The Apostle John explained this phenomenon in John 3:19-21: "Light has come into the world, but men loved darkness rather than light because their deeds were evil. Everyone who does evil hates the light, and will not come into the light for fear that his deeds will be exposed. But whoever lives by the truth comes to the light, so that it may be seen plainly that what he has done has been done through God."

"Impure hearts have an aversion for the light of truth; they love darkness," said St. Nektarios.

That is why Pascal said once that if you find you cannot believe in God, don't go around looking for more logical proofs of God's existence. Look rather into your heart. Extirpate the passions by God's grace. Repent of your sins. Let God purify your heart. For, only the pure in heart shall see God.

Without purity of heart, Satan will always be "displaying in us delusion in place of truth," said the Blessed Velichkovsky.

Personal Opinions Not Allowed

In talking with non-Orthodox Christians, an Orthodox bishop noticed that they usually began by saying, "I believe," "I feel," or "In my opinion."

At that point the bishop felt compelled to say to them, "Wait. It has no bearing on this matter what you believe, or think, or feel, or what my opinion is in this matter. The only thing that is of any importance and has authority in these matters is what the Holy Spirit has taught in the Church through the ages. In this, as in every matter, it is the Church and its Sacred Tradition, which includes the Bible, which must teach us, and we must listen humbly and be instructed. We do not make up our definitions of what Communion is, or who Jesus is, or of what God expects of us. These have already been defined by the Church in the scriptures under the guidance of the Holy Spirit."

"One must become as humble as dust before one can discover the truth," said Mahatma Ghandi.

We must yield humbly to God's Truth!

Truth is Not an Opinion

Truth is not an opinion or a fad. Like Jesus, it is "the same, yesterday, today, and forever."

Sometimes we worship opinions rather than truth. We would rather pay attention to 99 opinions because they are held by famous people than to the one fact we know to be the truth. Yet opinions are only opinions. They change.

Truth is truth. It never changes. It was true yesterday; it is true today; it will be true tomorrow. I would rather rest my life on one thing I know to be the truth than on 99 opinions, however famous the people who hold them.

Let's take an example. Consider what happens when we reject God's truth about sex. We begin to consider ourselves emancipated, free from all restraints. But consider how "emancipated" and "free" we are. Instead of following God's truth about sex, we begin to adopt the opinions of men and women whose attitudes towards sex are hardly normal in the first place. In other words instead of letting God tell us the truth about sex, we let other people, movie stars, football players, psychologists, etc., give us their opinions. We begin not only to follow but even to worship the opinions of these people.

So it happens every day. People forsake God's truth to follow the opinions of others. And the price they pay is horribly expensive. We need to heed the words of St. Ignatius of Antioch, "Indeed, you do not so much as listen to anyone unless his speech is of Jesus Christ in truth."

Where Do We Look for Truth?

Someone wrote,

> *I live from one tentative conclusion to the next, thinking each one is final. The only thing I know for sure is that I am confused"*

Contrast this confusion with what Jesus said:

> *For this I was born, and for this I have come into the world, to bear witness to the truth"* (John 18:37).

We have been told today, Who knows what is true or what is not true? What is true for you is not true for me! You have your truth, I have mine!

Frank Schaeffer wrote about the sad condition of truth in the U.S.,

> *The only absolute in modern America is that there are no moral absolutes, let alone absolute non-negotiable truths. One is free to believe anything personally, as long as one does not commit the faux pas of saying that it is true in an absolute or binding way that excludes falsehood or that would brand another philosophy as wrong. The very word orthodox is un-American. There are no orthodoxies in America, no right ways of doing things or believing. This relativistic worldview places the Orthodox, whether we acknowledge it or not, on a collision course with secular and most "religious" American society.*

This is another way of saying that most people in today's secular world have become atheists, not in the hostile antireligious sense of an earlier age, but in the sense that God no longer matters absolutely in their world.

The United States has suffered forty years of growing state atheism in the name of pluralism and multiculturalism. The result of this is that a subtle (and often no so subtle) de-Christianization and removal of religion from public life has occurred.

In the area of sexual promiscuity, TIME magazine reported that, "Just a short time ago, getting pregnant when you weren't married was the very worst mistake a 'nice' girl could make. Now, however, having a baby out of wedlock is kind of a status symbol."

Why is this happening? It's happening because there is a prevailing attitude that there is no right or wrong. And that is the same as saying that there is no such thing as truth. There is only one thing wrong with this.

Objective, Unchangeable, Eternal, Living Truth

There is truth—the objective, unchangeable, eternal, living Truth—Who is God. This is why Jesus Who is God-come-in-the-flesh said plainly, "I am... the Truth."

Jesus is the Truth that makes people free (John 8:32). and leads them to fulfillment and redemption. He is the Truth that brings us to fullness of life. He is the Truth about who we are and whose we are. He is the Truth about where we come from and where we are going. He is the Truth about why we are here and what life is about. He is the Truth about God, Who He is and what His will for us is.

To follow Jesus is to follow the Truth. To live in Jesus is to live not in half-truth or partial truth but in the fullness of God's Truth, divinely revealed in His Son and preserved in the Bible and in His Church.

Speaking of Jesus, Mother Teresa said, "Jesus is the Truth to be told... the way to be walked... the Light to be lit... the Life to be lived."

For us Orthodox Christians, Jesus is the Truth Whom we worship and in Whom we have placed our hope.

St. Augustine wrote, "Faith is to believe what you do not see; truth is to see what you have believed."

We see Truth in Christ. He is Truth Incarnate.

Truth Unveiled

The whole truth of who God is and who man is has been disclosed to the world in and by Jesus. That is why Jesus could say, "I am...the Truth."

One of the meanings of the Greek word for truth, alitheia, used by Jesus in this verse, is "without a veil." It is as if truth were wearing a veil before and now in Jesus the veil is removed and truth is revealed. Jesus is God with the veil removed.

As we read in Hebrews 1:1-2, "In many and various ways God spoke of old to our fathers by the prophets; but in these last days he has spoken to us by a Son, whom He appointed the heir of all things, through whom also He created the world."

God who had been speaking to our fathers through the prophets finally took off the veil and spoke to us in person through His Son, Jesus, through Whom the world was created and Who actualizes in His Person the Truth; the Truth the Greek philosophers sought as they walked the streets of the agora in Athens; the Truth that provides the answers to man's most vexing questions; the Truth about God, about man, about life, about death.

That Truth is Jesus!

St. Maximus explains that in the Old Testament we had the shadow of truth; in the New Testament we have the image of truth; it is only in the Kingdom of God that we shall have the complete truth: "For the things of the Old Testament are the shadow," he wrote. "Those of the New Testament are the image. Complete Truth is the state of things to come."

It is then that we shall see the Truth face to face. "Now we see but a poor reflection as in a mirror; then we shall see face to face. Now I know in part; then I shall know fully, even as I am fully known" (I Cor. 13:12).

Blow Out the Candles!

An ancient Chinese philosopher said once, "Blow out the candles! The sun is up!" The candles are the bits of truth discovered through the ages by the sages. They are candles when compared to the sun: Jesus, who as God is Truth Personified.

Orthodox Christians will not say that there are no truths in other religions.

St. Justin the Martyr taught that down through the ages God has been revealing fragments and crumbs of His truth to the Greek philosophers. "Wherever there is truth, it is the Lord's," he wrote.

Through the use of reason the early Greeks discovered several truths about God. Socrates, for example, even talked about the immortality of the soul.

Thus we believe that there are truths in other faiths. For wherever there is truth it has come from God. Yet these truths, scattered throughout the great religions of the world, are truths but not the Truth.

One Christian missionary to India wrote some years ago,

> I am convinced that while there are truths in all faiths, only Jesus is the Truth. He is the Word of Truth become flesh. The divine ideas which had wandered through the world, until they had forgotten their divine origin, did at last clothe themselves in flesh and blood. The great

theologian Karl Barth summarized this best of all when he wrote, "The truth of Jesus Christ is not one truth among others, it is the truth, the universal truth that creates all truth as surely as it is the truth of God... to know Him is to know all."

There are many religions, but only one Gospel.

Pascal wrote in his *Pensees,*

> *Not only do we understand God only through Jesus Christ, but we understand ourselves only through Jesus Christ. We understand life and death only through Jesus Christ. Apart from Jesus Christ, what we know is neither our life nor our death, neither God nor ourselves.*

"Apart from Jesus," someone said, "only the lie is truth."

And one wag added, "Everything is a lie. Just pick the lie you like best."

This is exactly what people are doing when they reject the truth of Christ. They just pick the lie they like best.

Permanency of Truth

When a famous theologian said once that the truth of Jesus is permanent, a scientist in the audience objected:

"No truth can ever be permanent," he said. The theologian asked, "Oh? When did science decide to have no integrity?" "Why," he replied, "integrity we have to have always." "Always?" asked the theologian. "And at what point do scientists now propose to have no concern, no concern for truth and no concern for life?" "Why," said the scientist, "concern for truth we always have to have." "Always?" asked the theologian. That was the end of the discussion.

There are some truths that are permanent because they are basic to life. No truth is more basic, more permanent than that which God gave us by revelation from above. There are some truths that just don't change. They are permanent. They are as absolute and unchanging as God is.

"Jesus is the same yesterday, today and forever."

If you think that "wrong" is only what you think it is, that it's only a word, listen to what Jesus said, "Think not that I have come to abolish the law and the prophets... For truly, I say to you, till heaven and earth pass away, not an iota, not a dot, will pass from the law until all is accomplished" (Matthew 5:17-18).

I remember being with a group of people, in casual conversation, when one person responded to a comment of another by saying, "But that would be wrong, wouldn't it?"

"Wrong?" the first one said with scorn in her voice, "There's no such thing as wrong! It's only a word! 'Wrong' is only what you think it is!"

After I heard this, I said to myself, "Isn't this one of the major reasons we are inundated by dishonesty, lies, and crime today?" *Wrong is only what you think it is!* It's only a word!

How can we not lament as we ask, *Whatever happened to truth?*

Some Things
Never Change

It seems that the rules today are changing only in the area of morals and values, only in the area of right and wrong.

The rules of science, for example, do not change. Water was H2O yesterday. It is H20 today. And it will remain H2O tomorrow and forevermore. If everyone were free to change the chemical formula of water, there could be no science.

Some things just don't change.

"Truth is the foundation of all knowledge," wrote John Dryden, "and the cement of all societies."

The Worship of Public Opinion

Polls have become for modern politicians what the oracle of Delphi was to the ancient Greeks: a mysterious and almost divine source of wisdom.

There are polls today for anything and everything: polls on what to wear to influence certain groups of people and what not to wear. There are polls on everything except how to behave with integrity, judgment, and honesty. Yet polls are not an "almost divine source of wisdom." Polls can be slanted in many ways by pros. This, of course, greatly increases the margin of error, which, in effect, is far greater than they say it is.

Following are some examples.

The Kinsey Report

Columnist Linda Charez wrote:

For nearly a half century, the name Alfred Kinsey has been synonymous with sexual freedom. In 1948, Kinsey published "Sexual Behavior in the Human Male" followed in 1953 by "Sexual Behavior in the Human Female" which revolutionized the way Americans regarded sex. Kinsey's data showed Americans to be far more sexually active and less faithful and more adventurous in their sexual practices than anyone had imagined. Indeed, it was Kinsey who first estimated that 10% of the male population is homosexual.

Now it appears Kinsey's "research" was more than a little suspect. For years, critics have pointed out that many of Kinsey's research subjects were prisoners whose sexual practices could hardly be viewed as typical. But the most damaging information has come recently from an unlikely source, the current director of the Kinsey Institute for Research in Sex, Gender, and Reproduction at Indiana University. John Bancroft, a psychiatrist who became Kinsey Institute director… admitted in an interview this fall that Kinsey relied for some of his most controversial data on child sexuality on information from a pedophile whose victims included 2-month-old children.

Yet, despite Kinsey's bizarre views and the tainted origins of his research, his polls have influenced the attitudes of two generations of Americans and remain to this day the most widely known and referenced data on American sexual behavior!

Whom Shall We Trust?

Every day we make choices about whom we are going to trust. Let's look at an example. An article a few years ago in a national magazine quoted a sociologist who had concluded, on the basis of some interviews, that infidelity could be good for marriage.

To buy that conclusion would be to walk as the world walks, trusting polls more than God. But God didn't leave any room for guesswork on this subject. He said plainly and unequivocally, "You shall not commit adultery" (Ex. 20:14).

Whom do we trust? One researcher, who asked 800 married men what they think? Or God, who created us, instituted marriage, and knows what is best for us?

The opinion of man—which is what the polls reflect—is no substitute for the Word of God.

Let's Vote!

I recall a story about children playing with a doll in a nursery. One child asked if the doll were male or female. They began to disagree violently until one child raised his hand and said, "Teacher, I know how we can find out."

"How?" asked the teacher.

The child replied, "Let's vote!"

Well, truth is never voted into existence by polls! Truth is reality. It is there. Whether we accept it or reject it, it is still truth.

And Truth for us Christians is a Person. "I am the Way, the Truth, and the Life," said Jesus.

Not Man's Gospel

St. Paul tells us that the gospel he received is not man's gospel. It did not come from man. It did not originate with any individual. It is not the result of any opinion poll. It was not born of the spirit of any "golden" age. It was not kicked out of a computer. It came "through a revelation of Jesus Christ" (Gal. 1:12).

Speaking at M.I.T. some years ago, Winston Churchill said that Christians have the blessings of a revealed religion.

Christianity is first and foremost a revelation. By revelation we mean that Christianity did not originate with man. It came from God. It was revealed to man from above. Our morals, our value system, our commandments, our guidelines, the principles we live and die by as Christians, come from God, not from man. They are revealed. They came "through a revelation of Jesus Christ."

As the Apostle Paul writes, "For I would have you know, brethren, that the gospel which was presented by me is not man's gospel. For I did not receive it from man, nor was I taught it, but it came through a revelation of Jesus Christ" (Gal. 1:11-12).

When God chose to give us the Ten Commandments, He did not ask the people to conduct a poll to come up with their favorite commandments. Instead Moses climbed

Mt. Sinai and there the Ten Commandments were given him by God engraved not on tissue paper but on stone tablets. The commandments did not come up from earth, from man; they came down from above, from God, by divine revelation.

Jesus said to Pilate, "This is why I was born; this is why I have come into the world: to bear witness to the truth" (John 18:37).

The truth Jesus revealed is a brilliant light for our minds, for He revealed to us "the secrets of the Kingdom of heaven." This is the light that shattered the darkness on the blessed night of the resurrection; the light that still appears at every midnight Paschal liturgy at the Tomb of Jesus in Jerusalem.

Pilate's Poll

Every Sunday in the Nicene Creed we mention Pilate, who, in the best tradition of democracy, went to the people and asked the "people" their opinion. He said, "I have two men in my custody. One of them, I am convinced is innocent of the charge against him, and the other is a proven murderer and a subversive. The innocent one is accused of calling himself the King of the Jews. The murderer is named Barabbas. Which one do you want me to release?" In other words, Pilate conducted an opinion poll!

And the people replied emphatically, "Barabbas! Barabbas!"

Thus, Jesus was crucified by the will of the majority! It was the public opinion poll of His day that placed Him on the cross. And is not His Truth, His law, still being crucified today by the majority through opinion polls?

It isn't polls or the public opinion of the moment that count. It is right and wrong. It is God's unchanging truth and His moral law.

Truth Distorted by Lying

Truth can be distorted by lying. What does God say about lying?

"Lying lips are an abomination to the Lord, but those who deal truthfully are His delight" (Prov. 12:22).

The Bible tells us that when God became incarnate in Jesus, He came as the incarnate Truth, the One Who was "the Way, the Truth, and the Life."

"God desires truth in the inward parts," says God's Word.

Jesus warned us that Satan's primary mode of operation is deceit. "He is a liar and the father of lies," said Jesus (John 8:44).

Furthermore, we see that when sin first entered this world, it did so embodied in a lie: "You shall surely not die if you eat of that tree," said Satan to Eve. He blatantly confronted God's truth with a lie.

In the New Testament when sin was first recorded in the Christian Church, again, it was enshrouded in a lie. Ananias and Sapphira held back a part of what they had promised to give to the Church, and then lied about it. Peter said to them, "Ananias, why has Satan filled your heart to lie to the Holy Spirit… You have not lied to men but to God." And then both were struck dead.

The ninth commandment says, "You shall not bear false witness to your neighbor." This is the sin of perjury.

Jesus said, "Let what you say be simply, "Yes", or "No"; anything more than this comes from evil" (Mt. 5:37).

In Matthew 12:37 Jesus said, "…by your words you will be justified, and by your words you will be condemned."

Is Lying Ever Justifiable?

Is lying ever justifiable? A Dutch woman faced this question years ago. If she revealed the truth that Jews were hidden in her father's house, she would be sending them to the gas chambers. If she lied, on the other hand, she would sin, but perhaps save them from death.

What should she have done?

She lied in order to save them. It was still wrong, but it was the lesser of two evils. She did it to obey a higher law, the law of love.

It is not that "the end justifies the means" or that morality is purely a matter of relativity. It is remembering the purpose of the law, which is to serve the highest law of love.

What is Wrong With Lying?

What is wrong with lying, distorting or denying the truth? The first thing that is wrong with lying is that one loses one's credibility.

When Aristotle was asked what a man could gain by telling a lie, he replied, "Never to be believed even when he speaks the truth."

Another person said, "What upsets me is not that you lied to me, but that from now on, I can no longer believe you."

Secondly, lying is wrong because it can become a sinful habit and thus a lifestyle. You begin to live the life of a lie, not even knowing that you are hurting others and offending God.

Hitler, for example, denied the truth and lost the war. He had a violent temper. In time, none of his officers dared tell him the truth about how the war was going, so all the news he received, up to the end almost, was good. When he finally learned the truth, the Third Reich was finished.

Thirdly, lying is wrong because relationships depend on truth. Unless others speak truthfully to us, we never engage real people but only phony images.

Unless we speak truthfully to others, we never experience the exquisite joy of being known and accepted for who we truly are.

Any friendship worth cultivating demands honesty. And honesty said Aristotle is "speaking the right truth to the right person at the right time in the right way for the right reason."

Fourthly, lying is wrong because, if we persist in it, we will end up lying to ourselves.

Confession essentially is being honest with God about ourselves. Confession entails overcoming self-deception, confessing and acknowledging the truth. I cannot move on to personal growth and fulfillment until I stop lying to myself and see myself truthfully in all humility and honesty as the sinner that I am.

Truth as a Compass

What does a compass do? Nothing. It just points the way. It points in one direction!

That is what Jesus does as the Truth. He points the way—the unchanging way. He points always in one direction—toward truth and freedom, for He Himself is Truth and Freedom.

Get the Right Pitch

A radio network received a letter some years ago from a prospector in the Montana hills.

"It gets lonely here," the man wrote. "I have a violin I used to play, but it's badly out of tune. Would you be kind enough to strike me the note 'A' Sunday night at seven, so I can put that fiddle back in tune?"

Amused by the odd request, network officials interrupted their scheduled program to comply.

A few days later, they received another letter from the prospector: "Many thanks. Now my fiddle is back in tune, and I'm not lonely anymore."

People today wouldn't even bother to ask for someone to give them the note 'A'. They no longer believe there is a standard, unchanging note 'A'. They make up their own note 'A'. And the result has been a horrible cacophony of moral rebellion and anarchy.

The Truth Stands
Before Zacchaeus

When people come face to face with Truth, Who is Jesus, miracles happen. This happened, for example, when Zacchaeus was confronted with Truth in the Person of Jesus (St. Luke 19:1-10).

This is how it happened.

Truth seeks out Zacchaeus hidden behind the thick leaves of a sycamore tree. Truth knows Zacchaeus' heart. He knows that Zacchaeus sincerely desires to see Jesus, so Jesus calls out to Zacchaeus. In response to Zacchaeus' desire to see Jesus, Truth invites Himself to Zacchaeus' house. "Zacchaeus, hurry and come down; for I must stay at your house today."

Standing in the Presence of Truth, Zacchaeus is convicted of his sinfulness and decides to do something about it. So, he says to Jesus, "Behold, Lord, the half of my goods I give to the poor; and if I have defrauded anyone of anything, I will restore it fourfold." In confronting Truth in the Person of Jesus, Zacchaeus confronts the truth about himself as a sinner.

Witnessing his repentance, the reparation he was willing to make to those whom he had defrauded, and his concern for the poor, Jesus said to him, "Today, salvation has come to this house, since he also is a son of

Abraham. For the Son of man came to seek and to save the lost."

But not all people respond to Truth the way Zacchaeus did. The Apostle John describes those who flee from the Truth just as Zacchaeus sought out and fled to the Truth (John 3:19-21).

A life kept holy and pure through daily repentance has much to do with acknowledging and accepting the Truth.

Since God is love, He cannot be known without love. And since He is pure, His truth cannot be known without purity of heart. "Blessed are the pure in heart for they shall see God (the Truth)," said Jesus.

The Poisoned Grain Crop

The following story expresses well what has happened to truth and to values in our society today:

Once upon a time in a distant kingdom, it happened that after the grain crop had been harvested and stored, it was discovered to be poison. Anyone who ate it went insane. The king and his advisers immediately took counsel as to what should be done. Clearly, not enough food was available from other sources to sustain the population. There was no choice but to eat the grain. "Very well," the king said, "let us eat it. But at the same time we must feed a few people on a different diet so that there will be among us some who remember that we are insane, and will remind us."

The purpose of the Church is to remind the world that its truth and values are insane, and to point the way to truth and sanity.

The Danger of Inner Emptiness

✠

Jesus told a parable about a house that was occupied by a demon. The demon was cast out, but the house remained empty. When the demon returned, he found the house empty, swept, and put in order. "Then he goes and takes with him seven other spirits more wicked than himself, and they enter and dwell there; and the last state of that man is worse than the first. So shall it also be with this wicked generation" (Mt. 12:44-45).

Denial of truth has created a vast inner emptiness, a nihilism, a nothingness, into which many evil spirits have entered. A house that is swept clean and emptied of God's truth is totally vulnerable to a multitude of demonic lies. Apart from Christ the lie becomes the truth.

When truth is proclaimed today, the world's quick response is "SEZ WHO?" If we have ears to hear the answer will come booming from above as it did in a recent cartoon: "SEZ WHO?" "SEZ ME!" saith the Lord.

The Truth of God is Unchangeable

"The word of the Lord abides forever" wrote St. Peter (I Peter 1:25). The truth of God abides forever because it is a revealed truth. We did not make it up, nor is it the result of an opinion poll. It came from God. It is unchangeable.

As Orthodox Christians we have the apostles' doctrine. It is the doctrine of Christ entrusted by Him to the apostles which is carefully guarded by the Apostolic Tradition and exists as the deposit of faith in the Church. In other words, this is the truth, the doctrine the apostles learned from the Lord, which they in turn passed on to their followers, always within the Church which is the bulwark and guardian of truth.

The Nicene Creed, for example, is one of the most beautiful and complete descriptions of our faith ever written. It is our magna carta as Orthodox Christians, the distilled essence of what the apostles taught and wrote as recorded in the New Testament.

We first received the Creed at holy baptism. We believe it. We live it. We confess it. We preach it. But we don't try to streamline it. We don't re-write it. We don't re-design it to fit the twenty-first century.

It is fixed, unchangeable, eternally true. Truth—God's Truth—abides forever.

The Nicene Creed: Truth Unchanged

Clark Carlton writes in his book *The Way: What Every Protestant Should Know About the Orthodox Church*:

> ...the Nicene Creed has been read or sung by the Orthodox Church unchanged since its adoption roughly 1600 years ago and will continue to be guarded inviolate until the Lord "shall come again in glory to judge the living and the dead." Those who enter the loving embrace of Holy Orthodoxy do so with the confidence that She will not alter the parameters of Her faith established by the Apostles and the holy Fathers or diminish the deposit of faith. As the Eastern Patriarchs wrote (to the English non-jurors) in 1718, "We preserve the Doctrine of the Lord uncorrupted, and firmly adhere to the Faith he delivered to us, and keep it free from blemish and diminution, as a Royal Treasure, and a monument of great price, neither adding anything, nor taking anything from it." In free church Protestantism, on the other hand, anything which constrains the individual—even the truth—is viewed as a threat to his autonomy. It is no wonder then that Baptists have such a phobic reaction to the historic creeds of the Church. The fact that the Nicene Creed and other conciliar definitions of the Church exist threatens the free church Protestant. Why? Because they bear witness to a faith that is not a

matter of individual opinion and is not subject to revision. The content of those symbols [creeds] is a threat because it is the negation of the very foundation of Protestantism itself: the individual. *

It is not the Church, the Body of Christ, that defines truth but the individual, according to Protestantism.

Clark Carlton goes on to say:

When I encountered the Orthodox Church, I was confronted with the truth—the truth about God, about the world, and about myself...

When I embraced the truth of Orthodox Christianity...I rediscovered the Bible—not as a magic book that fell out of heaven, but as the Book of the Church, the divinely inspired record of God's revelation to man...

When I embraced Orthodoxy...I embraced the Church...which is "the pillar and ground of the truth" (I Tim. 3:15). *

It is the Church—not the individual—that is the pillar and foundation of truth.

---

* *The Way: What Every Protestant Should Know About the Orthodox Church.* Clark Carlton. Regina Press. Salisbury, MA. 1997.
* Ibid.

Heretics Change the Truth

St. Irenaeus (Second century) described the heretics as those who were constantly changing the truth. He wrote:

> *All heretics are like this. They imagine that they have found something higher than the truth...They set off on all kinds of uncertain paths, holding now one opinion, now another, on the same subject! They are like the blind who lead the blind and rightly fall into the ditch of ignorance at their feet. They are always seeking, but they never find the truth... Their thoughts soar above the permitted measure of thought. That is why the apostle says: "Do not think more loftily than you ought to think, but think prudently" (cf Rom. 12:3). He is warning us not to taste the knowledge of the Gnostics, which "thinks more loftily than it ought to think", and leads to our banishment from the "paradise of life".*

Truth is Not Moderately Important

G.K. Chesterton said once that the only reason for believing in Christianity is because it is true: "Christianity is a statement," he said, "which, if false, is of no importance, and, if true, is of infinite importance. The one thing it cannot be is moderately important."

If you are about to drink something and someone tells you that it is poisonous, that truth cannot be moderately important. It is of infinite importance.

Even more so is the truth about who God is, who you are, why you are here, where you are going, and the existence of heaven and hell. These truths are not moderately important but of infinite importance. They affect us personally and existentially, both for now and for all eternity.

Truth as Dogma

The Church uses the word "dogma" to signify a fixed, unchanging truth about God.

Science, too, has dogmas, i.e., water is H2O, 2+2=4, etc. These are dogmas or unchanging truths.

The word "dogma"—truth—appeared only when heresy—untruth—began to threaten divinely revealed truth.

Christos Yannaras tells us that "the word 'heresy' means the choice, selection, and preference of one part of the truth to the detriment of the whole truth, the catholic or universal truth."

Heresy, thus, is the opposite of catholicity (wholeness). In other words, the heretics were dealing not with the whole truth but with half-truths. They took a half-truth and passed it off as the whole truth as Arius did with the person of Jesus, claiming that Jesus was the Son of Man but not the Son of God. The Church proclaimed the whole truth, the Catholic truth, that Jesus was both God and man in one and the same Person.

We know that there is not a greater or more dangerous lie than a half-truth. That is why the Church, using dogmas and the Nicene Creed, defined truth and established its boundaries once and for all.

And because—as was already stated—it was the Eastern Church that took the initiative in establishing the boundaries of truth through the first Seven Ecumenical Councils, it came to be known as the "Orthodox" Church, or the Church that preserves the wholeness or catholicity of the deposit of faith entrusted to the Apostles by our Lord, without adding or subtracting from that original deposit.

Today, however, dogma is a bad word because it implies to the secular, unbelieving world, that there exists such a thing as absolute, unchanging truth. Some even say that there cannot be any heresy today because there is no longer any dogma (absolute truth) from which to stray.

Contrary to what some believe, however, dogmas do not imprison the truth. They set truth free by defining it and establishing its boundaries.

International Bureau of Weights and Measures

In the town of Sevres, a suburb of Paris, is the head-quarters of the International Bureau of Weights and Measures, an organization that standardizes units of measure. The bureau establishes standards for metric measurements, and ensures a reliable standard for physical measurements around the world. If I wanted to obtain the most precise measurement possible, I would refer to the standard they maintain. If I wanted to be absolutely certain that the millimeter divisions on my ruler were accurate, I would compare them against the bureau's standards.

Now, suppose you and I had a dispute about a length of canvas I had cut for you. I measured it and told you it was one meter long; you measured it with your own meterstick and pronounced that it was less than one meter. How could we determine who was right? We could appeal to the standard; there exists an objective and universal standard in Sevres, France.

Just as we have an International Bureau of Weights and Measures, so we have a standard for right and wrong, a standard for truth and untruth. That standard has been established by God in Christ. He is the Truth. He is the standard, the model, the plumb line of truth. And your local Orthodox Church with its presbyter and bishop is the Intercosmic Moral Bureau of Weights and Measures for Truth with a capital "T". Not my truth or your truth but God's Truth.

The Truth is Christ

William Temple said once, "The ultimate truth is not a system of propositions grasped by perfect intelligence but a personal Being apprehended by love."

The Person who is ultimate Truth is Jesus.

C.S. Lewis wrote,

> *I know, Lord, why you utter no answer.*
>
> *You are Yourself the answer.*
>
> *Before Your face questions die away.*

Mother Maria of Normanby wrote,

> *Truth for us is not a system of thought. Truth is not created. Truth is. Christ is the truth. Truth is a person. The search for Truth is the search for the person of Christ.*

There is a fixed and timeless standard by which all things are measured and judged. That standard is the Lord Jesus.

If two plus two equals four, then Jesus is the "four", the only right answer when it comes to God and truth. All other truths or answers must be measured according to their proximity to, or remoteness from, the Truth Who is Jesus Christ.

No other religion makes the stupendous claim that "the Word became flesh and dwelt among us" (John 1:14).

And that "Christ is the image of the invisible God and the first-born of all creation" (Col. 1:15).

A religion that makes such claims cannot be equated with any other faith. It demands that we invite all people to this faith for salvation (The Great Commission Matt. 28:1-20).

When the Bible says of Christ, "in Him all things hold together" (Col. 1:17), it is telling us that: Jesus is the glue that holds everything in the universe together.

Consider the following questions: Why is there something instead of nothing? Why do we see design in the universe? Why is water always H2O? Why are so many processes in nature so deeply connected?

It is because "in Him (Christ) all things cohere, hang together." Jesus is the One who holds the universe together. Jesus is the clue that solves the puzzle. He is the infinite Who defines the finite. He is the absolute that makes sense of it all. For without an absolute, there can be no right or wrong, no morals, no values. Without an absolute we are left only with opinions. Without an absolute we are left with nothing but half-truths and lies. Without an absolute the lie becomes the truth.

St. Isaac wrote, "Satan is a name denoting the deviation of the human will from truth." The same St. Isaac of Syria wrote, "Knowledge of truth fills the heart with peace, establishing a person in joy and confidence."

The Greek Philosophers Were Really Seeking Jesus of Nazareth

Charles Malik, former President of the U.N. and a devout Orthodox Christian wrote,

In his tremendous speculations about the teleology of the universe, Aristotle was really seeking Jesus of Nazareth, and if only he had met him, he would have understood why that is so. In his insistence on a supreme and beneficent "good" behind all phenomena, full of solicitude for humankind, Plato was really seeking Jesus of Nazareth, and if only he had met him, he would have understood why that is so. In his wonder about the nous (mind) behind the order of the universe, Anaxagoras was really seeking Jesus of Nazareth, and if only he had met him, he would have understood why. All people of ambition—the conquerors and scientists and philosophers, the industrialists and statesmen, the celebrities and media moguls—are really seeking Jesus of Nazareth, and if only they would meet him, they would understand why. Every alienated person who is profoundly unhappy with himself and with the world, every drug addict trying to escape the burden of existence, every prostitute who does not realize what is happening to her, every victim of terminal illness facing the grave in terror of the unknown, is really seeking Jesus Christ of Nazareth, and if he or she would only meet him, he or she would understand why.*

---

* *The Wonder of Being.* C. Malik. Word Books. Waco, TX. p. 119

Ultimate Questions

There are ultimate questions that have tormented people since the world began: Who is God? Who is man? What is our purpose in life? What is behind the cosmos? Why are we subject to pain and death?

All these ultimate questions find their complete answer only in Christ Who is the Fullness of Truth. The answer does not come through the efforts of a brilliant mind but through God's gracious revelation in Christ.

Fr. George Florovsky called the Bible "the very icon of truth" because it brings Christ to us.

Evelyn Underhill wrote, "That which we know about God is not what we have been clever enough to find out, but what God's love has secretly revealed in Christ."

Truth Through a
Personal Relationship
With Jesus

The late saintly Bishop Gerasimos Papadopoulos
emphasized that truth is apprehended through a
personal relationship with the Lord Jesus; for Jesus who
is Truth, is also love.

> *For Christian faith, truth is not simply rational,*
> *philosophical knowledge and scientific achievement. It*
> *is knowledge of the very Person of Christ. We need to*
> *know Christ Himself and not something about Christ.*
> *Christ Himself is truth itself. The truth in the Person*
> *of Christ is known as a personal relationship and*
> *communion with Christ in a mutual love, for a person*
> *is known only in a personal relationship*.*

To know Jesus we need to love Him as much as Fyodor
Dostoyevsky did when he wrote:

> *Sometimes God sends me moments in which I am*
> *utterly at peace. In those moments I have constructed*
> *for myself a creed in which everything is clear and*
> *holy for me. Here it is: to believe that there is nothing*
> *more beautiful, more profound, more sympathetic,*
> *more reasonable, more courageous and more perfect*
> *than Christ, and not only is there nothing, but I tell*
> *myself with jealous love that there never could be.*

---

* *Reflections of Our Christian Faith and Life.* G. Papadopoulos. HCO Press. 1995.

A Bold New Image
of Christ

Recently a contest, offering a $2,000 prize, invited artists to create a bold new image (icon) of Christ to mark the 2000th year of His birth. The major specification was that the image of Christ be something entirely new that had never been seen before. Any image that in any way resembled an existing image would be rejected.

This contest reflected the secular world's rejection of the one, true, historic Christ, and its search for a Christ whose truth would be more palatable to the secular standards of today's world.

It turned out that the award-winning image was submitted by a female non-believer from Santa Fe, New Mexico. The painting was an appalling image of New Age correctness. It portrayed Jesus with a woman's body, black face, and vacant, drug addicted eyes. Yet it was this painting, replete with yin and yang signs and Indian feathers, that was selected by a Roman Catholic magazine to be the 21st century image of Christ!

Christ is no longer "the same yesterday, today and forever." Every century must create its own Christ in its own image.

Truth Speaks

Speaking to us as the Truth, Jesus made some awesome statements about Himself:

I am the Alpha and the Omega (Rev. 1:8).

I am the door: if anyone enters by me he will go in and out and find pasture (John 10:9).

I am the Bread of Life (John 6:35).

I am the Light of the world (John 8:12).

I am the Resurrection and the Life (John 11:25).

I am the living water that springs up to eternal life (John 4:14).

I am the Good Shepherd (John 10:14).

I am the Way, the Truth and the Life (John 14:6).

I am the light shining in the darkness which the darkness cannot overcome (John 1:5).

Whoever believes in Me, even if dead, will live and whoever lives and believes in Me will have eternal life (John 11:25).

These are not the statements of a mere man. No wonder, it was said of Him, "No man ever spoke as this man."

Syncretism

The Bahai temple in Wilmette, Ill., expresses the Bahai belief that all religions point to the same ultimate reality.

The temple has nine magnificent porticoes, each dedicated to the prophet of one of the world's major religions. Like spokes on a wheel, the porticoes lead to a single central altar via nine radial aisles. The altar symbolizes the one God at the center of the many religions. It doesn't matter by which portico you enter or which aisle you take. All lead to the same place.

The Bahai temple is an architectural expression of a widespread belief: Although the religions of the world seem different, they are all equally valid ways to the same truth.

This is no longer simply a belief of the Bahai or some other sect, however. It is comfortably at home in American culture, given our democratic sense that all are equal.

Yet, how can all religions be equally valid ways to the same truth when they teach opposite and contradictory truths?

Buddhism teaches that the goal of life is emptiness (Nirvana) while Christianity teaches that the goal of life is not emptiness but fullness, i.e., "to be filled with all the fullness of God" (St. Paul). Theosis.

Hinduism teaches that there is no forgiveness, only karma and repeated re-incarnations. No one can escape paying the penalty of sin. Christianity, on the other hand, offers forgiveness, grace, and new life, through a Savior on a cross.

Islam teaches that the books of the Christian Bible were lost and that what we have today is not the Bible, but a complete distortion of God's word.

They teach furthermore that it was not Christ who died on the cross, but someone else who took his place.

They teach that anyone who believes that Jesus is God is a blasphemer and will be condemned to hell.

Do these contradictory teachings sound to you as if all religions are equally valid ways to truth?

Do We All Believe in the Same God?

Contrary to what some believe, we do not all "believe in the same God."

The Jehovah's witnesses do not believe in our God. The Hindus do not believe in our God. The Mormons do not believe in our God. The Christian Scientists do not believe in our God.

Nor do we believe in their God.

Blessed Augustine wrote, "Christ is to be found only in name among some heretics who wish to be called Christians, but in truth, He is not to be found in any of them."

Not One Truth Among Many

A young man told me one day that he believed in Jesus Christ, but then he added, "However, that does not mean that I do not believe all of the other religions are good and valid. I do not go along with the theory that Jesus is the only way."

The trouble with this statement is Jesus Himself.

God said, "I am Who I am." He did not say, "I am whoever you think I am."

Jesus said, "I am the way, the truth, and the life. No one comes to the Father except through me" (John 14:6). (See also Matthew 16:13-17.)

He did not say, "I am one alternative among many, and all roads lead to the same God." He did not say, "I am whoever you want me to be."

All Roads Do Not Lead to God

Contrary to what some people believe, all roads, meaning all religions, do not lead to the same God. We all try to scale the same mountain but many go up the wrong side and never make it to the top. We choose a slope that does not lead to the peak.

History records many famous accidents on the Matterhorn: whole groups of mountaineers roped together and crashing down on the rocks.

There is a right way and a wrong way to climb the Matterhorn. So it is with our climb to God. We need to go up the right way, on the right road and with the right guide. And that Guide for Orthodox Christians is none other than the Lord Jesus Christ. He is "the way."

"There is salvation in no one else, for there is no other name under heaven given among mortals by which we must be saved" (Acts 4:11-12).

St. Paul wrote,

> He (Jesus) is the image of the invisible God, the first-born of all creation; for in Him all things were created, in heaven and on earth, visible and invisible, whether thrones or dominions or principalities or authorities—all things were created through Him and for Him.

He is before all things, and in Him all things hold together.

He is the head of the body, the church;

He is the beginning, the first-born from the dead, that in everything He might be pre-eminent.

For in Him all the fullness of God was pleased to dwell (Col. 1:15-19).

The Man in the Pit

The difference between Christ and all other religions is best illustrated by this story:

A man fell into a deep, vile, filthy pit in which there was a huge serpent.

Along comes an Animist. He looks down into the pit and sees the serpent. His eyes open wide and he flees into the jungle lest the same evil spirit should heave him into the pit.

Then comes a Confucianist and he says, "Ah, so! Great man never fall in pit. Walk circumspectly and henceforth you will look where you walk."

A Hindu comes along and says, "Ah, my brother, you *think* that you are in a great black pit, but it is the error of your mortal mind.

The fact is that all is Brahman and Brahman is all, and this external world is merely illusion.

The pit does not exist. Think, 'There is no pit, there is no pit, there is no serpent,' and all will be well... peace." And he leaves.

A Muslim happens along next and says, "I will help you, my friend."

He reaches down and grabs him by the arm and pulls him halfway out of the pit. Then he draws his knife and says,

"However, you will become a Muslim won't you?" "I can never do that," answers the man, and back into the pit he goes.

A Buddhist looks down and says, "Dear friend, you are suffering greatly in the pit and the reason you are suffering is because you want to get out of the pit. It is your desire that is making you miserable. What you must do is come to a cessation of all desire and then you won't mind being in that pit." And he walks away.

And then comes Jesus! He looks with compassionate eyes at the man in the pit and into that foul and dirty hole He leaps between the man and the serpent, which rears its ugly head and strikes at the Saviour, sinking its fangs into His side. As the venom of the serpent flows into the blood of Jesus, with His last strength, He lifts the man out of the pit.

Therein lies the difference between Christianity and all other religions!

Confucius died and was buried. Buddha rotted with food poisoning. Mohammed went the way of all flesh, leaving behind a harem. But Jesus Christ rose from the dead and by His resurrection, He demonstrated that He was indeed the "Son of God come with power."

By His life, death, resurrection, ascension and future second coming, Jesus declares that He is the incarnate God Himself, "the way, the truth, and the life."

Other religions may have bits of truth. But only Christ has, or rather, is the Fullness of Truth.

There are many religions, but only one Gospel.

The Basic Difference

A Moslem and a Christian were discussing their religions and had agreed that both Mohammed and Christ were prophets. Where, then, lay the difference?

The Christian illustrated it this way: "I came to a crossroads and I saw a dead man and a living man. Which one did I ask for directions?"

The response came quickly. "The living one, of course."

"Why then," asked the Christian, "do you send me to Mohammed (or Buddha) who are dead, instead of to Christ Who is alive?"

Is not this the basic difference between Christ and every other religious leader? All the others came into the world, lived and died—but none of them came back from the dead and lives on.

The resurrection of Christ was the one event that persuaded His disciples once for all that Jesus was indeed God in the flesh and not just man.

The Elephant and the Blind Man

Let me share with you a fable. Six blind philosophers inquire into the nature of an elephant. One falls against its side and thinks the elephant is like a wall. The second blind philosopher feels the tusk and thinks the elephant is like a spear. For the others, the trunk is like a fan, and the swinging tail is like a rope. The blind philosophers each think that their distinctive experience represents the truth.

The fable suggests that each of the world's great religions thinks its experience of the ultimate reality is the truth. But superior wisdom, according to this logic, teaches the "real" truth, namely, that each religion has only part of the truth. Its mistake is in thinking that it has the whole truth!

The Christian looks at the fable and realizes that the six blind philosophers represent the non-Christian religions of the world, groping in the darkness for the light, the truth about God. The Lord Jesus Christ, Who is Truth Personified, restores our sight. He opens our eyes so that we many see the whole picture, the entire elephant, and thus come to the knowledge of truth. Apart from Christ we are indeed blind and see only a small part of the truth as do the non-Christian religions. But in Christ, with eyes opened, we see the entire truth for "in Him [Christ] dwells the fullness of God," says St. Paul.

He is indeed not part of the Truth, but the whole Truth.

The Gift of Discernment

In order to discover truth, Scripture and the Church Fathers insist that we need God's guidance through the gift of discernment (*diakrisis*).

Discernment is the gift of God's special wisdom that enables us to distinguish between good spirits and evil spirits, truth and falsehood, since evil spirits invariably disguise themselves to appear as "angels of light." Discernment is important because the devil is the father of lies. He distorts truth and creates delusions and fantasies in us.

The Apostle John calls on us to test every spirit to see if it is of God (I John 4:1-3).

The term "discernment of spirits" is found in I Cor. 12:10 where St. Paul lists "discerning the spirits" as one of the gifts of the Holy Spirit.

Discernment is often called the third ear or the third eye. To be able to distinguish truth from falsehood, we need the gift of discernment, which is one of the charisms of the Holy Spirit and abides in the Church. This is especially true in today's secular society which has dethroned God's truth and where each person is encouraged to invent his own truth.

Diakrisis, or discernment, is called "the queen of all virtues" by Sophronios of Jerusalem.

The monastic tradition of the Church has always recognized the need for discernment. The spiritual fathers of the desert were well aware of our tendency to deceive ourselves and to follow our own desires, instead of the will of God.

Guidelines for Discernment

Discernment needs to be based on certain criteria or guidelines. Such criteria do exist in the Church. Here are some:

Conscience is one such guideline. St. John Chrysostom wrote, "Open the doors of your conscience and see the judge seated in your mind."

The Holy Bible is another guideline that lays before us the divinely revealed will and truth of God.

Another guideline to help us discern truth are the ethical rules of the Church. Fr. Stanley Harakas writes, "The ethical rules are the accumulated wisdom of the Church. They serve to save [us] continuous expenditure of time and energy in deciding anew each situation."

Still another excellent resource that will help us distinguish truth from falsehood is our spiritual father.

St. Mark the Ascetic, urges his spiritual son, Nicholas, to:

> *make an effort to keep company with, and be with and be under the guidance of experienced spiritual fathers. For it is dangerous living alone, on one's own, without supervision or with persons inexperienced in spiritual warfare...for the deviousness and treachery of evil is great...*

Fr. Stanley Harakas emphasizes the importance of consulting with spiritual fathers for ethical decisions. He writes,

> When a decision is difficult, there is need for counsel and the consultation of those who are informed and ethically sensitive in the spirit of prayer. "That which is obscure," says St. Basil, "can be more easily discerned by the earnest scrutiny of several persons, since, to be sure, God grants issue to the quest under the guidance and counsel of the Holy Spirit, according to the promise of our Lord Jesus Christ." In making decisions, we need to have the assistance of other Christians, our Pastors, spiritual Fathers, and the teaching Church.

The Church Fathers keep emphasizing that he who chooses himself as a guide has chosen a fool.

Another guideline that will help us discern truth is prayer. Discernment of spirits is a gift of the Holy Spirit which is granted to us by prayer. This calls for living in a state of constant prayer in order to maintain an ever-present openness to the Spirit's guidance.

God has promised to give us the Holy Spirit to guide us into all truth (John 16:13).

Thus, the gift of discernment which enables us to distinguish truth from falsehood, and what is of the Holy Spirit from what is of the unholy spirits, manifests itself as:

1. Conscience, the voice of God within us praising us when we do right and chastising us when we do wrong.

2. The Holy Bible which is "a light unto my path and a lamp unto my feet."

3. The ethical rules of the Church which constitute the accumulated wisdom of the Holy Spirit abiding in the Church and teaching us through the centuries.

4. Our spiritual father who embodies the Spirit of God and is a friend and counselor.

5. Prayer which invites the Holy Spirit to come and pitch His tent in us. Thus, the gift of discernment is best called *prayerful* discernment.

6. Purity of heart which cleanses the eye of the soul enabling us to see God and His holy will. "Blessed are the pure in heart for they shall see God," said Jesus. Sin beclouds our vision of God and truth.

St. Gregory of Nyssa said, "Every passion bears within it the seed of death since it dulls the spirit of discernment."

For effective discernment to take place, the heart must be kept in a purified state through daily repentance.

Nepsis (Vigilance) Begets Diakrisis (Discernment)

Discernment is one of the many benefits of growing in vigilance or watchfulness.

Bishop Kallistos Ware explains how this happens,

> *Growing in watchfulness and self-knowledge, the traveller upon the Way begins to acquire the power of discrimination or discernment (in Greek, diakrisis). This acts as a spiritual sense of taste. Just as the physical sense of taste, if healthy, tells a man at once whether food is moldy or wholesome, so the spiritual taste, if developed through ascetic effort and prayer, enables a man to distinguish between the varying thoughts and impulses within him. He learns the difference between the evil and the good, between the superfluous and the meaningful, between the fantasies inspired by the devil and the images marked upon his creative imagination by celestial archetypes.*

When movies such as Pocahontas offer us in animated form a religion, animism, which is nature worship; when a book on the N.Y. Times Best Seller List, quotes the Bible and talks about Jesus and the importance of prayer, but turns out to be nothing but New Age teaching dressed up in Christian terminology, denying Jesus and His basic teachings; when New Age people write books wherein the authors purport to have private chats with God and place their own words in God's mouth; with all of this going on, we would be lost without the spirit of discernment which enables us to "test this spirits to see whether they are of God" (I John 4:1).

---

* *The Orthodox Way*. Kallistos Ware. SVS Press. Crestwood, N.Y. 1981.

Truth as Mystery

One of the greatest Christian thinkers of the twentieth century, Dr. Mortimer Adler, author, teacher, philosopher, and intellectual giant is best known, perhaps, for his work with the Great Books series of the classics of Western culture.

In 1984 Dr. Adler became a Christian. Explaining why he became a Christian, he wrote: "My chief reason for choosing Christianity was because the mysteries were incomprehensible. What's the point of revelation if we could figure it out ourselves? If it were wholly comprehensible then it would be just another philosophy."

Adler goes on to describe his creed: "Articles of faith are beyond proof. But they are not beyond disproof.

We have a logical, consistent faith in the world. But there are elements to it that can only be described as mystery."

Adler mentions the three main mysteries of the Christian tradition: the Trinity, the Incarnation, and the Resurrection. "Your faith and my faith must include these three mysteries. They are difficult to understand. They are not unintelligible—God understands them. But for us there is an element of mystery." Then Adler concludes: "The greatest error anyone can make is to think they can fully understand these three mysteries. It makes a mockery of faith."

Clement of Alexandria said, "If someone expects to comprehend all things merely through his physical senses, he has fallen far from the truth."

Orthodoxy has always acknowledged the mystery that is involved in the truths of our faith. They are not against logic but beyond logic. Faith takes over exactly at the point where reason and logic end.

Our sovereign God is beyond logic. If God could be totally understood, He would not be God.

"My ways are not your ways," says the Lord.

Hence truth in Christ is surrounded by an aura of mystery which keeps us forever humble before His awesome truth. But to the prideful modern mind, said Flannery O'Connor, "mystery becomes a great embarrassment."

The Rock of Faith

As Christians we stand neither on the rock of science, nor on the rock of logic, but on the rock of faith, which is also the rock of truth.

St. John Chrysostom expressed it this way.

> *The sea is surging and the waves are high: but we have nothing to fear because we stand on a rock—the rock of faith. Let the sea surge with all the power at its command, and let the waves rise as high as mountains; the rock on which we stand will remain firm and unshaken. Do I fear death? No, because on the rock of faith I know that death is the gateway to eternal life. Do I fear exile? No, because on the rock of faith I know that I am never alone; Christ is always beside me, my friend and my brother. Do I fear slander and lies? No, because on the rock of faith I know that I am always protected by the truth—Christ, who is the truth, is my protector. Do I fear poverty? No, because on the rock of faith God also provides for my needs. Do I fear ridicule? No, because however low I may sink in the esteem of those without faith, on the rock of faith all are treated with respect. Far from fearing the surge of the sea, I enjoy it, because it assures me that the rock on which I stand is immovable.*

Jesus Who is Truth is also "my rock and my salvation" in the words of the psalmist. He is my immovable rock, my unchanging Truth, my eternal salvation. The truth revealed by Christ enables me to stand firm on the rock of faith.

Science and Truth

The late Bishop Gerasimos Papadopoulos wrote concerning the relationship of truth in science and faith:

> *True science and true theology can never come into conflict in their search for truth... Christian truth is not the result of human science; it is truth received [from God] by divine revelation... Science has its limitations, and where it stops faith takes over. While science cannot enter the realm...of faith, Christian truth can illuminate the free work of science and provide for it some directions for thought and research.**

We need to remember that science attempts to answer the *how* questions of the universe, *how* galaxies formed, *how* hemoglobin came about, *how* life began, but science should have virtually nothing to say about the *who* question. *Who* made it all? *Who* is the designer and creator?

Answering the *who* question is beyond the realm of science. It is the Book of Genesis that answers the question *who*.

Science, on the other hand, tries to answer the *how* questions. *How* did God create water? *How* did He create rocks?

If religion sticks with the *who* question as does the Bible, and, if science sticks with the *how* questions, there should be no conflict between religion and science.

---

* *Reflection on Our Christian Faith and Life*. G. Papadopoulos. HCO Press. 1995.

Behind every door of science one meets God and how He has been at work in the universe.

The Bible is not a book of science. It does not concern itself with how the world was created or how old it is. The Bible answers the questions science can never answer, the *who* question. *Who* created the universe? *Why* did He create us? *Who* is God? *Who* are we in His eyes? *How* does He look upon us?

There should never be a conflict between the truth of God and the truth of science. The truth of God complements the truth of science. The truth of science elucidates the truth of God.

The great scientist, Sir Isaac Newton, said once,

> *I do not know what I may appear to the world; but to myself I seem to have been only a boy playing on the sea-shore, and diverting myself in now and then finding a smoother pebble or a prettier shell than ordinary, whilst the great ocean of truth lay all undiscovered before me.*

The true scientist is kept humble, like Sir Isaac Newton, because he knows that no matter how much he has learned, there will always be "a great ocean of truth" out there yet to be discovered.

A Right and Wrong Way

There is a right and wrong way to do everything. There is a right and wrong way to sing. There is a right and wrong way to swing a golf club. There is a right and wrong way to bake a pie. There is a right and wrong way to live.

Living is a science based on definite laws. If you do not obey those laws, life will go badly for you. When you learn those laws and obey them, you are set free to enjoy the gift of life and to use it for God's glory.

"The truth will make you free," said Jesus. But first you must know the truth, love the truth, obey the truth, respect the truth, and submit to the truth.

It is very easy to reject the truth. When a person does not want to believe, he can always find a way to deny the truth. Countless are the people who live in a state of denial.

"It is so easy to deny the existence of the sun," said St. Chrysostom. "Just close your eyelids and there is no sun, only darkness."

Who is it Who Finds the Truth?

Socrates was walking by the water one day when a young man asked him, "Socrates, may I be your disciple?" Socrates didn't say anything; he merely started to walk into the water.

The young man followed, asking again, "Socrates, please let me be your disciple." But Socrates answered not a word and kept walking into the water.

The young man still followed, pleading "Socrates—" At that point Socrates turned around, grabbed the young man by the hair, pushed him under water, and held him there until he knew he could take no more.

The man came up gasping for air. Socrates looked at him and said, "Young man, when you desire truth as much as you desire air, then you can be my disciple."

There is a price to pay for truth. And the price is total commitment to Jesus as God. We shall find the truth if we are willing to empty ourselves of pride and stand before God in utter nakedness and humility. We shall find the truth if we are willing to "deny self, take up our cross and follow Him."

We shall find the truth if we love Jesus with our whole being, for God, who is Truth, is love. And He is apprehended by love.

We shall find the truth if through repentance we let God cleanse our hearts and minds that we may see His truth clearly, "Blessed are the pure in heart, for they shall see God."

There is a direct relationship between truth and purity of heart. Only the pure in heart can see God and come to know His Truth.

When we want Jesus more than anything else in life, truth will be His gift to us.

The Mirror of His Truth

The truth of God is like a mirror.

The Apostle James writes,

For if anyone is a hearer of the word and not a doer, he is like a man who observes his natural face in a mirror; for he observes himself and goes away and at once forgets what he was like (James 1:23-24).

The truth will make us free, but first it may make us miserable as we look into the mirror of God's truth and see ourselves as we truly are: sinners in need of God's cleansing and forgiveness.

As the Truth, Jesus confronts each one of us with the truth about ourselves. And this may not always be pleasant. One person wrote,

I remember being at a retreat once where the leader asked us to think of someone who represented Christ in our lives. When it came time to share our answers, one woman stood up and said, "I had to think hard about that one. I kept thinking, "Who is it who told me the truth about myself so clearly that I wanted to kill him for it?" According to John, Jesus died because he told the truth to everyone he met. He was the truth, a perfect mirror in which people saw themselves in God's own light.

And because they did not like what they saw in the mirror of God's truth, they crucified Him.

Is He not being re-crucified today for the same reason? Whatever happened to truth?

Let me put it a little more personally: What is happening to truth in your life right now? Is it being crucified through denial, suppression and a thousand excuses, or rather lies? Or has truth transformed you through repentance into "a new creation" who is glorifying God?

Winston Churchill said once, "People occasionally stumble over the truth, but most of them pick themselves up and hurry off as if nothing had happened."

What Do We See in the Mirror of Truth?

As we look into the mirror of God's truth what do we see? What do we learn about ourselves? Do we like what we see? Do we see our sin? Truth is not always pleasant.It can cut like a surgeon's knife.

Master Surgeon that He is, Jesus can use truth to cut out of our life all that is false and wrong, all that is dishonest, unfair, unloving, inauthentic, and untrue.

But first we must repent, admit and confess the truth about ourselves. We must allow Christ to change us, to transform us into the image of His likeness.

Is not this the purpose of truth? Not to talk about it intellectually, not to admire it from afar, but to accept it and let it transform us.

Carlo Martini, Archbishop of Milan, put it this way:

> We are all seeking truth, and so am I. We desire truth. We look for it, ask for it, want it at every moment of our life. And if I had to explain this search, I would explain it, at least in my case principally as a desire for authenticity. Before the Lord I want to be authentic and that means I want a correspondence between my words and my actions.*

We pray that the truth of Christ may produce such authenticity in us.

---

* *Journeying With the Lord.* C. Martini. Alba House, N.Y. 1987. p. 486.

Facing Up to Truth Personally

As the only creature capable of doing wrong, man is the only one capable of telling himself that wrong is right and evil is good.

Man, the only creature capable of reasoning, is the only creature capable of denying truth, devising all sorts of rationalizations and excuses for what he does.

Dr. M. Scott Peck, author of the book *The Road Less Traveled*, wrote, "Evil is the persistent refusal of the evil person to face the truth about himself. He is constantly scapegoating, laying it on other people, projecting his sins onto others."

But if man is a self-excusing animal, he is also more than an animal. He is created in the image and likeness of God. As such he is far more than an animal.

Animals do not repent, but man can and must repent. He can face up to the truth about himself, face up to what he can become when he receives God's forgiveness. For no other creature has been destined to be a partaker of God's nature.

The Apostle John says it clearly, "If we say we have no sin, we deceive ourselves and the truth is not in us" (I John 1:8)... "If we say we have not sinned, we make Him (God) a liar and his word is not in us" (I John 1:10).

All this passing of the buck—says Apostle John—is nothing but deceit, a lie, a denial of reality.

But the Apostle John goes on to say, "If we confess our sins, He (God) is faithful and just, and will forgive our sins and cleanse us from all unrighteousness" (I John 1:9).

Those who deny their sin, their accountability, are self-deceived, says the Apostle John. They deny truth.

David was not self-deceived when he said, "Against Thee, Thee only, have I sinned and done evil in Thy sight." Because he faced the truth of his sin, he experienced the joy of God's salvation.

Where Does Man Turn When He Denies God's Truth?

When man denies God's truth he turns to various forms of madness for guidance.

St. Mark the Monk (5th century) wrote, "As a result of the fall of man, error became more characteristic of human beings than truth."

When God is denied, movie stars become our new "saints" as do sports heroes. Denying God's truth, we look for it on TV talk shows or soap operas or in opinion polls.

Denying God's truth leaves us open prey to any cult leader who comes along to impose upon us his "truth" (read untruth or lie) in order to enslave us. Having denied God's truth, the United States has become a prime mission field for thousands of cults and sects.

Denying God's truth, many turn to nihilism. This is the philosophy of nothingness, euphemistically known as tolerance, which Dorothy Sayers describes as follows:

> *In the world it is called Tolerance, but in hell it is called Despair...the sin that believes in nothing, cares for nothing, seeks to know nothing, interferes with nothing, enjoys nothing, hates nothing, finds purpose*

in nothing, lives for nothing, and remains alive
because there is nothing for which it will die.

Denying God's truth, others turn to astrology. The daily horoscope (read horrorscope) replaces the Bible. Our future is determined by the location of the stars. In place of the glorious freedom given to us by Christ, we allow ourselves to become tyrannized and victimized by the stars. Denying the guidance of God, we accept the guidance of inanimate stars.

By the way, when someone asks me what my "sign" is, I love to reply by drawing the sign of the cross on a piece of paper and saying, "This is the sign I was born under, baptized under, live by, and will die by." Not the sign of Aquarius but the sign of the cross. The sign of the One 'who loved me and gave Himself for me'; the sign of the One Who cares for me and guides me. It is Him I consult each day through prayer, the Church, and His word—not the stars."

There is no end to the tragic foolishness of man when he denies the truth of God.

I like what Kathleen Norris wrote, "I go to church to get away from the lies our culture gives us."

G.K. Chesterton put it this way, "The Church is the one thing that saves a man from the degrading servitude of being a child of his time."

Truth Creates Responsibility

Cicero said, "It is impossible to know the truth and not be held responsible."

Truth involves more than being persuaded of truth. It involves loving truth. Love without truth is false; truth without love is ingenuine.

To be transmitted effectively, Christian truth needs to be packaged with love and delivered with love.

"Speak the truth with love," wrote St. Paul.

Why? Because the God of truth is the God of love.

An Imprisoned Romanian Priest Testifies to the Truth

When Truth (Christ) is loved, it will be proclaimed boldly, as boldly as did a Romanian Orthodox priest who was imprisoned by the communists for his faith in Christ.

A fellow prisoner told the following story about him.

There was a brigade in Romania which was only for priests, bishops, pastors, rabbis, and laymen - whoever was in prison for his faith. One day a political officer came to inspect that brigade. Everybody stood at attention, and at random he called out a young man (whose name was Coceanga) and asked him, "What have you been in your civilian life?"

And he replied, "Sir, what I have been in my civilian life, I will be forever. I am a priest of God."

"Aha, a priest! And do you still love Christ?"

The priest was silent for a few seconds - seconds as long as eternity, because he knew that his eternal destiny would be decided in those seconds. The Lord said, "Whoever confesses Me before men, him I will also confess before My Father who is in heaven. But whoever denies Me before men, him I will also deny before My Father who is in heaven" (Matthew 10:32, 33).

And then after a little meditation, his face began to shine - I have seen so many shining faces - and with a very humble but very decided voice he said, "Captain, when I became a priest, I knew that during Church history thousands had been killed for their faith. And as often as I ascended to the altar dressed in those beautiful, ornate robes, surrounded by the respect and love of the congregation, I promised to God that if ever I had to suffer, if ever I wore the uniform of the prisoner, I would still love Christ.

"Captain," he went on to say, "I so pity you. We have the truth, and you have whips. We have love, and you have iron bars and prison cells. Violence and hatred is a very poor argument against truth and love. If you were to hang all the professors of mathematics, how much would be four plus four then? It would still be eight. And eight plus eight would still be sixteen.

"You can't change the truth by hanging those who speak the truth. if all the Christians were hanged, it would still remain so that there is a God, and He is love. And there is a Savior; His name is Jesus Christ, and by confessing Him a man can be saved. And there exists a Holy Spirit, and a host of angels around the earth. And there exists a beautiful paradise - you can't change the truth."

I wish there was a way to convey the tone with which he said those words. We, the others, were ashamed because we believed in Christ, we hoped in Christ, but this man loved Christ as Juliet loved Romeo and as the bride loves the bridegroom*

If we are possessed by Truth, we will proclaim it (Jesus) boldly.

---

* *Again Magazine.* Conciliar Press. Ben Lomond, CA Vol 23. No. 2

God holds us responsible for what we do with truth (hence the final judgment at the Second Coming of Jesus).

Reminding us that God will hold us responsible, St. Paul writes, "The wrath of God is revealed from heaven against all ungodliness of men who by their wickedness suppress the truth…" (Rom. 1:18).

Truth means sharing it with the world: hence the Great Commission: "Go therefore and make disciples of all nations, baptizing them in the name of the Father and the Son and the Holy Spirit, teaching them to observe all that I have commanded you…" (Matthew 28:19).

Speaking of the man in the parable of the talents who had hidden his one talent in the ground, St. Ambrose said, "Equally at fault is anyone who could share the truth but keeps it to himself."

Sharing the truth means bearing witness to the Truth. It means living a life consistent with Truth, an authentic life. It means that where there is error, we are to sow truth.

Truth has consequences. Ignore the Truth and the consequences are deadly. Embrace the Truth and the consequences are salvation and eternal life with God.

We Are All Responsible for Truth

According to the teachings of the Orthodox Church each member of the Church—not just the bishops, not just the priests, but *everyone* is responsible for truth.

If anyone sees something they consider not to be in the spirit of the Bible and the Tradition of the Church, they need to speak up.

Truth had to be fought for in the tradition of the Church and countless martyrs accepted death rather than betray the Truth. Passion for truth produced the great Church Fathers.

And the great Ecumenical Councils through the Holy Spirit preserved and handed down the truth to us whole and in tact. Truth had to be studied and discussed and debated under the guidance of the Holy Spirit in the Councils of the Church before it was clarified.

For, as John Cassian said, "Truth always shines brighter when it is ventilated (through discussion)." And truth was ventilated in the Apostolic Council as well as the first seven Ecumenical Councils.

Truth is like a lighted lamp in that it cannot be hidden away in the darkness because it carries its own light.

Though often crucified, it is ultimately resurrected.

St. Maximus the Confessor: A Martyr for Truth

Maximus the Confessor, for example, paid a heavy price for upholding the truth of Christ. Thrown into prison, his tongue was cut off so he couldn't speak, and his hands were cut off so he couldn't write. He died in prison. Twenty years later a consensus of the faith decreed that Maximus was right. He was then canonized and named Saint Maximus the Confessor.

The early Christians not only confessed the truth of Christ, millions of them suffered and died for the truth as martyrs. St. Maximus the Confessor was martyred for truth.

The Greek word for martyr (*martys*) means an eyewitness, one who is an eyewitness to something. This indicates the revelatory aspect of martyrdom. A martyr is a public witness who makes the truth visible in his or her life.

As the powers of darkness seek to extinguish the light of Christ, the martyr makes it shine from within the darkness of death and violence.

There is always a price to pay for truth. It does not come cheap.

The Family and the Church

The two institutions that can teach the truth most effectively are the family and the Church. These are the "communities of memory" to which Robert Bellah refers where traditions and history are preserved.

The most effective place to teach the truth of Christ is in the family by God-fearing parents. It is for this reason that St. John Chrysostom called the home the "little church".

It seems, however, that the family and the church have now been replaced by television as the transmitter of truth. The United States has undergone a severe moral "dumbing down" during the last few years. In this moral "dumbing down" television regularly portrays people with low standards of behavior as not only normal but also decent. What children see on television becomes for them normal behavior. Television becomes their tutor and gives them a "mind", not the "mind of Jesus" but a sick mind, the mind of the world. And the result is a sick society where children bring weapons to school and shoot to kill.

The family and the church need to assume their God-given role as the "communities of memory" where truth is preserved and passed on.

The Christian family finds the truth in the Church, "the pillar and foundation of truth" (I Tim. 3:15).

St. Irenaeus (2nd century) wrote about the Church as the preserver and keeper of truth:

> *We do not need to seek the truth elsewhere; it is easy to obtain it from the Church. In the most thorough way, the apostles have amassed in the Church, as in a treasure, all that pertains to the truth, so that everyone who so desires may drink the water of life (cf. Apoc. 22:17). She [the Church] is the entrance to life; all the others are thieves and robbers (cf. John 10:8). We must, therefore, reject them but love with the greatest zeal everything to do with the Church and lay hold of the tradition of truth.*

The Orthodox Christian faith is not founded on beautiful thoughts.It is anchored firmly on truth, on God's word, as preserved in the Church. It is founded on objective fact, on decisive historical events that occurred during the time when Augustus and Tiberius ruled Rome. It stands or falls on the reality of those events. It is founded on the reality of the resurrection of Jesus.

St. Paul's letter to the Corinthians puts the matter starkly: "If Christ has not been raised, then our preaching is in vain and your faith is in vain."

Judgementalism
and Truth

Sociologist Alan Wolfe refers to what he calls America's new eleventh commandment: "thou shalt not judge." This refusal to judge comes from the belief that there is no real, objective truth any more. Something may be true for you but not for me! So why judge other people and their ideas?

William J. Bennett responded to such thinking when he wrote, "Those who constantly invoke the sentiment of 'Who are we to judge?' should consider the anarchy that would ensue if we adhered to this statement in, say, our courtrooms. What would happen if those sitting on a jury decided to be 'nonjudgmental' about rapists, and sexual harassers, embezzlers and tax cheats? Justice would be lost.

Without being 'judgmental' Americans would never have put an end to slavery, outlawed child labor, emancipated women or ushered in the civil rights movement.Nor would we have mobilized against Nazism and Communism... for it is precisely the disposition and willingness to make judgments about things that matter that is a defining mark of a healthy democracy."*

---

* *The Wall Street Journal.* March 5, 1998. "Why It Matters." Wm. J. Bennett

If there is real objective truth, then that truth must sit in judgment upon error.

If there is light, then light must sit in judgment upon darkness.

If everyone's truth is equally valid, then there cannot be any judgment.

But if God has spoken His truth in Christ, then we are all liable to judgment.

"It is appointed unto men once to die. Then comes judgment" (Hebr. 9:27).

The Holy Spirit grants us the gift of discernment that we may judge, but always with love and great discernment. To be able to discern correctly what is true, we need to have spiritual ears that are constantly open to the Holy Spirit.

Jesus, the Demons, and Truth

Writing of the devil as the "father of lies", Paul Evdokimov says:

> *While for Plato the opposite of truth is error, for the Gospel, at its deepest level, it is the lie. "Liar and father of lies" by essence, the Evil One has taken upon himself a frightful vocation, that of knowingly altering truth. The initial perversion of his will has made it possible for him to usurp whatever he can in order to fabricate an existence with spurious materials. Isaiah clearly describes this enterprise: "We have made lies our refuge, and in falsehood we have found a hiding place" (Isaiah 28:15).**

St. Athanasius warns that we are not to believe the demons even when they speak the truth:

> *He [Jesus] put a bridle in the mouths of the demons that cried after him from the tombs. For although what they said was true, and they did not lie when they said, "You are the Son of God" and "the Holy One of God", yet He did not wish that the truth should proceed from an unclean mouth; and especially from such as those who under pretense of truth might mingle with it their own malicious lies.*

---

* *Ages of Spiritual Life*. Paul Evdokimov. SVS Press. Crestwood, N.Y. 1998. p. 90

Euthymius writes that truth becomes mere bait for the demons who speak the truth only to deceive:

> He [Jesus] has taught us never to believe the demons, even when they say what is ostensibly true. For since they love falsehood, and are most hostile to us, they never speak the truth except to deceive. They make use of truth as a kind of bait.

A Basic Quest

One of man's basic quests in life is to find the truth. One of the first questions we ask when we come into the world is "Why?"

As children, we tear apart our toys to find out what makes the wheels go round. As grown-ups we tear apart the universe with telescopes and microscopes and satellites to find out what makes it go round.

Yet he who seeks the truth is really seeking God, who is the lodestar of all truth.

"There is no more pleasant food for the soul than the knowledge of truth," said Lactantius.

"Why am I here? Who am I? Where am I going? What is my purpose in life?"

People who ask these questions are really seeking God.

The large number of religions in the world indicates how much people hunger and thirst for truth, i.e., for God.

The Need for Apologists

An example of a person whose quest for truth led him to Christ is Justin the Martyr. As one of the Greek philosophers, he was a great seeker after truth. He had studied all the philosophies of his day: the Stoics, the Peripatetics, the Pythagoreans, the Platonists, etc. In each of them he had found bits of satisfaction but not the inner satisfaction of the final answer to life.

One day a Christian introduced him to Christ. Justin began reading the Bible in earnest. As he came to know Christ he found in Him the complete and final answer to life. His quest for truth as a philosopher was satisfied completely by Christ.

He became a Christian—the first of the philosophical scholars and theologians of the early Church who defended the faith. He became an apologist for the faith.

Justin insisted to the end on remaining a "philosopher"—a "friend of the truth" for he had found in Jesus both a Friend and the Truth.

Christianity as a Countercultural Movement

By becoming a Christian, Justin felt he had become a better philosopher. He was now able to study all the truths discovered by various philosophers and make sense of them within the framework of the one perfect Truth provided by divine revelation in Christ Jesus. He believed that pagans understood reality only in part, since Christ was the fulfillment of all the partial truths embodied in pagan philosophy.

The Church today desperately needs apologists like St. Justin. Christians who will give a reason for their faith.

For the Church today needs to become a countercultural movement in order to resist the blatant lies that are offered as truth.

The early Christians were countercultural as they stood up and opposed the world.

In the words of St. Paul, "...become blameless and pure, children of God without fault in a crooked and depraved generation, in which you shine like stars in the universe, as you hold out the word of life..." (Phil. 2:14-15).

Two Plus Two Equals Four

As was stated previously, it has become fashionable today to say that all religions are equally true. To think that yours is better is the height of rudeness. Yet consider the following incident.

The Dalai Lama recently urged his followers not to worship a certain god because it turned out that that god was discovered to be an evil spirit.His followers protested. They liked that god. They wanted to continue worshipp ing him. They are threatening to break away from the Dalai Lama.

The Dalai Lama himself had been worshipping this false god all his life. Now he discovers that this god is an evil spirit.

Who can say, in view of this, that all religions are but different roads leading to the same God? To do so, one would have to discard logic.

The Truth of Christ: Empirically Tested

T he reality of the Truth of Christ can be tested empirically. Consider the following example.

An agnostic, who held no beliefs about God, once challenged a Christian leader to a debate on the subject, "Agnosticism versus Christianity." The Christian leader agreed on one condition: the agnostic must first give evidence that agnosticism was beneficial enough to be worth defending. He must bring one man who had been a reprobate (criminal, drunkard, etc.) and one woman who had been trapped in a degraded life, and show that both people had been rescued from their plight by embracing agnostic unbelief.

Meanwhile, the Christian leader would bring to the debate 100 men and women who had been amazingly changed from a terrible past by believing in Christ.

The skeptic withdrew his challenge, unable to find even one person who had been transformed by unbelief.

The Truth of Christ is not abstract. It can be tested empirically in lives that have been made new in Christ.

"God Spoke! God Spoke!"

A Hasidic story tells of a disciple who asked his teacher what the secret of joy was.

The teacher told the story of a disciple who came each day to hear his master read the Torah. The Torah is the Law and Word of God that is found in the first five books of the Old Testament.

As the Hasidic master read from the Bible the words, "And God spoke..." the young disciple jumped up and ran, exclaiming over and over in exuberant joy, "God spoke! God spoke! God spoke!" as he danced Zorba-style.

That, said the master to the disciple, that is the beginning of joy.

God has indeed spoken. He has spoken the ultimate Truth in the Person of Christ. He continues to speak the truth to us through Jesus in the Bible and the Church.

And that is the beginning of joy—eternal joy! Unending joy!

Falsehood Disguised as Truth

St. Paul writes in 2 Cor. 11:14: "Satan disguises himself as an angel of light."

Falsehood can also disguise itself to appear as truth.

In fact, there is an old legend found in one of the odes of Horace. It tells how Truth and Falsehood went swimming together. According to this legend Falsehood stole Truth's clothing, and Truth preferred to go naked rather than appear in the garments of Falsehood. This is how the phrase "naked truth" originated.

Truth refuses to wear the garments of Falsehood but Falsehood never hesitates to wear the clothes of Truth. Just as the devil wore the mask of a serpent to deceive the first man and woman, so he wears thousands of seemingly innocent masks today to deceive us.mHe transforms himself into "an angel of light" so that he may present to us falsehood as truth and truth as falsehood.

One of the early church fathers said, "Something can sound very logical and still be false" (Mark Felix).

This is how the Anti-Christ will deceive many in the last days.

As St. Irenaeus wrote in *Against Heresies*:

> *Error, indeed, is never set forth in its naked deformity, lest, being thus exposed, it should at once be detected. But it is craftily decked out in an attractive dress, so as, by its outward form, to make it appear to the inexperienced (ridiculous as the expression may seem) more true than the truth itself.*

The Need for Vigilance

The Fathers of the *Philokalia* emphasized the importance of nepsis, vigilance, because they believed that the arch-enemy of the soul is a certain kind of thought which they described with the word *logismoi*.

Logismoi essentially are a train of thoughts that befog and pollute the mind so that bit by bit the mind drifts away from reality into a world of demonic fantasy.

In the writings of the Desert Fathers, *logismoi* are thoughts caused by demons.

Such thoughts are the seeds of the passions, those impulses that emerge from the subconscious and soon become obsessive.

Logismoi are important because all battles are won or lost first in the internal dialogue of the mind. The greatest battles are fought in the minds and hearts of people. For example, virtue is natural to us, while vice is unnatural. Yet, vice is made to appear far more attractive than virtue because the *logismoi* step in, and, backed by demons, they darken the mind, preventing it from seeing the beauty of virtue, while they clothe vice with an artificial attractiveness.

Falsehood wears the garments of truth, while truth refuses ever to wear the garments of falsehood and goes around naked.

In the Sorrows and Joys of Life Listen to Him!

A llow me now to apply the truth of Christ personally to you. When the burdens of life become too much for you; when it seems as if you cannot take it any longer, listen to Jesus as He says to you, "Come to Me all you who labor and are heavy laden and I will give you rest."

God is speaking His Truth to you personally and lovingly! Accept it.

When you are so filled with anxiety that your days and nights are replete with gnawing fears, listen to Jesus Who says, "My peace I give to you, not as the world gives do I give you."

God is speaking His Truth to you personally and lovingly! Accept it.

When sorrow fills your days and nights with despair, listen to Him Who says, "In the world you have tribulation; but be of good cheer, I have overcome the world."

God is speaking His Truth to you personally and lovingly! Accept it.

When guilt racks your conscience so that you can no longer live with yourself, come to Him Who is waiting to say to you, "Thy sins are forgiven, go and sin no more!"

God is speaking His Truth to you personally and lovingly! Accept it.

When you are confused as to which way to follow, which road to take, listen to Him Who says, "I am the Way, the Truth and the Life. No man comes to the Father but through me."

God is speaking His Truth to you personally and lovingly! Accept it.

And your life will be transformed.

Archimedes: A Place to Stand On

Archimedes, the Greek philosopher, was once asked how much he could lift? Having discovered the fulchrum, he replied, "Give me a place on which to stand and I can lift the world."

The place on which to stand is Jesus the Christ, Who is the Way and the Truth. Standing on Him we can indeed "lift the world."

St. Paul had discovered this truth. That is why he wrote, "I can do all things through Him (Christ) who strengthens me."

"Give me a place to stand and I can move the world."

That place, that most solid of all foundations is the truth of Christ.

Rejoice in the Truth

God has indeed spoken the truth. A truth that redeems. A truth that liberates. A truth that saves. A truth that delivers us from sin and death. A truth that establishes the kingdom of God within us. A truth that leads to unending joy.

So, like that young Hasidic disciple: Rejoice! Dance if you wish.

For, finding the Son of God, Jesus, means finding: Truth. Wisdom. Virtue. Justice. Life. Freedom. Joy. Redemption. Life Eternal.

To Jesus Who is Truth personified—the Son of the Living God—together with the Father and the Holy Spirit be all honor, glory, praise and thanksgiving now and forevermore.

Two Prayers

Lord, keep us from vain strife of words:
Grant to us a constant
Profession of the Truth.
Preserve us in the Faith,
True Faith and undefiled,
That ever we may hold fast
That which we professed when we were Baptized
Unto, and in the Name of the
Father, Son, and the Holy Ghost.

- St. Hilary of Poitiers (368 A.D.)

The second prayer is from the Liturgy of St. John
Chrysostom:

Grant us in this world, O Lord,
the knowledge of Thy truth,
and in the world to come,
life everlasting.

Orthodoxy stands for truth in faith.

Objective, absolute truth in today's secular

society is nonexistent.

Postmodernism has taught the world

that truth is relative.

What is true for you is true for you.

What is true for me is true for me.

This book is a must for all Christians

especially for young people

in higher education where

the only absolute truth is that

there is no "absolute" truth.

ABOUT THE AUTHOR

Anthony M. Coniaris

Rev. Anthony M. Coniaris, was born in Boston, Massachusetts in 1926, and attended Boston Latin School and subsequently graduated from Holy Cross Greek Orthodox Theological Seminary in Brookline, Massachusetts. Coniaris received a Masters of Divinity from Northwestern Theological Seminary in Minneapolis, and continued studies in the fields of religion and psychiatry at the University of Minnesota and at St. John's University in Collegeville, Minnesota.

Coniaris served as pastor of St. Mary's Greek Orthodox Church, from 1953 – 1992 – his only parish assignment. After his retirement in January 1993 he devoted most of his time to Light & Life Publishing Company which he founded in 1968. He authored more than 75 books, pamphlets and brochures. Light & Life became one of the largest distributors of Orthodox materials in the world. He also lectured at retreats and seminars at several Orthodox parishes in the US as well as in Canada. In addition, Coniaris was an Adjunct Professor of Homiletics at Holy Cross Greek Orthodox Seminary in Brookline, Massachusetts and taught there during his retirement.

He is past President of the Minneapolis Ministerial Association, the Twin Cities Metropolitan Church Commission, the Minneapolis Professional Men's Club, the Minneapolis Kiwanis, and the Greater Minneapolis Council of Churches. He was a member of the Board of the Children's Heart Fund, and was listed in WHO'S WHO in

RELIGION 1976-77. He received the WCCO Good Neighbor Award in 1973 and the Alumnus of the Year from Holy Cross Seminary. In 2018, he was awarded the Degree of Doctor of Divinity from Holy Cross Greek Orthodox School of Theology.

He passed away at the age of 93 in 2020.

....

Available titles authored by Anthony M. Coniaris

Introducing the Orthodox Church

My Daily Orthodox Prayer Book

Making God Real in the Orthodox Christian Home

Let's Take A Walk Through Our Orthodox Church

Your Baby's Baptism in the Orthodox Church

Nicene Creed For Young People

Surviving the Loss of a Loved One

Confronting and Controlling Thoughts

Philokalia: The Bible of Orthodox Spirituality

A Beginner's Introduction to the Philokalia

Tools for Theosis

God & You: Person to Person

Discovering God

Christ's Comfort for Those Who Sorrow

....

LIGHT + LIFE PUBLISHING
WORLD'S LARGEST ORTHODOX SUPPLIER

Light & Life Retreats & Seminars©
Learn to Live the Orthodox Faith

Is your church looking for a retreat leader who can present ancient Orthodox truths in a practical and contemporary fashion without watering down the wisdom of our Church? Our Light & Life presenter, Daniel Christopulos, is available for retreats, seminars or lectures prepared from the following Light & Life publications authored by our beloved Fr. Anthony Coniaris. The three books below are topics for the currently offered Light & Life Retreats & Seminars©:

Tools for Theosis ~ Becoming God-like Through Christ

God and You: Person to Person

Making God Real in the Orthodox Christian Home

Fr. Anthony Coniaris is the Founder and President of Light & Life Publishing Company and has authored over eighty-five books and pamphlets. Presenter Daniel Christopulos has served many years in US Orthodox parishes, been an Orthodox missionary in Africa where he taught at the Archbishop Makarios III Seminary in Nairobi, Kenya, taught at the high school, college and university levels, and been a national trainer for the US Department of Health and Human Services Office of Adolescent Pregnancy Programs. He currently is the US Country Representative for International Orthodox Christian Charities (IOCC) where he has worked since 2001.

Retreats are tailored to your specific time frame in full-day (9am–3pm) or a day-and-a-half format (typically Friday night and all day Saturday). Lectures, seminars and other longer retreats can also be designed to fit your parishes' spiritual needs.

For more details, please email patty@light-n-life.com or call 952-200-9566. We look forward to partnering with you in strengthening the spiritual life of your church.